AS IF IT MEANT

SOMETHING

As If It Meant Something

STEVE DENEHAN

RENARD PRESS

RENARD PRESS LTD

124 City Road
London EC1V 2NX
United Kingdom
info@renardpress.com
020 8050 2928

www.renardpress.com

As If It Meant Something first published by Renard Press Ltd in 2023
For previous publication details of individual poems please see p. 276

Text and cover illustration © Steve Denehan, 2023

Design by Will Dady

Printed in the United Kingdom by Severn

ISBN: 978-1-80447-029-9

9 8 7 6 5 4 3 2 1

Renard Press is proud to be a climate positive publisher, removing more carbon
from the air than we emit and planting a small forest. For more information
see renardpress.com/eco.

Contents

AS IF IT MEANT

SOMETHING

For my family and friends,
and for Will, for taking a chance.

One of Those Days

There has been rain
lots of it
all morning

wind, too, hard and bellowing
slamming the house
corrugating the canal

no yellow, no blue
just grey and dark grey
Monday May 10th, 2021

Long and Thin,

from Her Temple to Her Jaw

We went to lunch sometimes
she would talk and I would listen
while looking at the ducks
in the pond on Stephen's Green

she came into work once
with a bruise
on the side of her face
it ran, long and thin
from her temple
to her jaw

I asked her what had happened
without hesitation she said
that he had pushed her
into the side of the wardrobe

it was not the first time
it was not the last
I told her to leave him
she told me that she loved him
I asked her how
she smiled

we sat on a park bench
eating our sandwiches
finding silence in the noise
the ducks swam back and forth
eventually, she spoke
'If you don't laugh, you'll cry,'
she said, as she did neither

The Murder Face

The Murder Face
that is what they call it
my wife and daughter
snickering behind their hands

they always ask what I am thinking of
when I have *the Murder Face*
I always tell them
that I do not know
which is true
sometimes

though sometimes
it is a lie
I do know
I know exactly
I have been thinking of what
given half a chance
I would do to the guy
who is tailgating me
to the woman in the queue
standing far too close behind me
breathing on my neck
her open-mouthed chewing
almost inside my ear
to the cashier who rolls her eyes and tuts
when I mention
that she has left me a fiver short

grim thoughts
that do not appear in my mind as a lightbulb
but rather seep
inky, sticky, warm, black
from the edge
to the centre
to my face

they say it again
The Murder Face
they laugh
I laugh
I laugh along
I laugh along right along with them

Broken Nail

I asked her what had happened
she looked down
sighed
said that it had broken so easily
maybe brittle from the cancer
maybe brittle from the treatment

I asked if there were other side effects
she smiled wistfully
her hair was thinning
she had a hell of an itch all over
couldn't sleep
said that she was lucky

though we both knew that was not true
it was eating her
from the inside out
lungs
ovaries
diaphragm

she asked about my parents
my daughter, my wife
only getting breathless once
she looked down at her broken nail again
said that it would grow back
I didn't know what to say to that

Metallic

It had been building for a few weeks
the pain
forgettable initially
bulletproof eventually

the dentist stood over me
shaking his head
talking of bridges, caps and root canals
I shook my head
having been down those roads before
with mixed results
in that it had gone badly
or very badly

he looked horrified
when I told him to take it out
said that we could save it
as though it were a limb
or my sight
not a furious, rotten tooth
hidden in the dark of my mouth

he got down to it
pulled and twisted
pulled again until

driving home I tasted blood
warm and metallic
oddly familiar
my tongue ventured cautiously
a tentative slug
I wanted to know
I didn't want to know
and then, I felt it
what I knew that I would feel
nothing
nothing at all

Desert Cars

It is like a sea
is a sea, really
glinting under the California sun
cars, three hundred and fifty thousand cars
driven to the desert
parked in lines, rows
shimmering, perfectly uniform
Volkswagens
mostly black, grey and silver
the odd red

worth hundreds of millions
they are left to rot
to be taken by the elements
and eventually
by the land
something to do with emissions
and deception

maybe some day
after centuries, after millennia
fall as grains of sand
in an egg timer
there will be no desert
but lush forests
maybe in one section trees will struggle
or grow crippled and mutated

maybe our distant descendants
will study the soil
find toxins
find rust

maybe they will dig
until the shovels jar in their hands
until they hear a dull thud

they will speculate
wonder why
a kind of religion…
a form of worship…
some kind of mass grave…
but with no answers
no way of knowing
they will look at each other
and scratch their heads
much as I do now

anonymouse_weezil

I ate the back of my hand last night
in a half-dream
half-nightmare

everything was vivid
besides the pain
of which there was none

the flesh was all texture and no taste
a gelatinous resistance
to my teeth and tongue

I saw the long, thin bones of my hand
moving smoothly up and down
as though seeing the workings
of a clock
with no face

online, I discovered
that there are experts for dreams
but not nightmares
people detail their dreams on a forum
receive analytical responses
are grateful
for a stranger's insight
into their own subconscious

there are dreams of falling, murder
car crashes, drowning, being buried alive
I found just one instance of someone
eating their own hand

the analysis they received
speaks of a crisis of identity
a fear of losing the sense of self
or of being consumed by ambition
or obsession or a tendency
towards self-destruction or a yearning
to be a better communicator

each dream expert has a different explanation
often contrasting and conflicting
always vague
until anonymouse_weezil wrote
'Maybe it's just a fuckin dream.'
which, in the end
is what I went with

Cherry Red

She followed love to Paris
but love soon left her

she could dance, she was desperate
the clothes came off
the francs piled up

a burlesque queen, an exotic dancer
an artist, an ar*tiste*
never, ever
a stripper

it paid the bills and she kept a distance
no contact of any kind
during or after
she became adept
at gracefully avoiding
drunken, leering lunges

the call came and, with both hands
she took it
a stand-in dancer
at Moulin Rouge
six sparkling months
the best of her life
a golden time
in a golden era

* * *

She looks at herself in the mirror
ninety years old now: somehow
her skin is soft but the lines
are deep and they are plenty
there is still fire
she sees it
in her eyes, two jewels
at the bottom of a laundry basket
her hands shake slightly
as she paints her lips
cherry red, her signature shade
she opens the door
walks out
strips, with all that grace
her clothes
from the washing line
humming softly
to herself and no one else

Fingerprints Are
Snowflakes

I do not have a criminal record
have never had to *roll, not press*
the pad of my finger on an Indian ink sponge
then down on to a crime sheet

I was adopted and so
have two mothers
and two fathers
none of whom
could separate my fingerprint
from any other

I have a laptop
state of the art
with an on/off switch
that doubles
as a fingerprint reader

it turns on
flutters to life
just for me
every morning
when I touch it
a miracle of technology

magic
science fact from science fiction
we are connected
in this intimate way
the laptop and I

it is Tuesday morning, January 27th, 2021
I sit down on the couch
into a cyberpunk dream
I press the button while remembering
that fingerprints are snowflakes
both unique and both
eventually
will disappear

Broken Vacuum Cleaner

His vacuum cleaner broke today
the final straw
the tipping point
a small thing, really
but enough

he called me
his voice, ice cracking
on a sunshine day
said he knew
that it was just a vacuum cleaner, but

with his body failing him
and his mind leaving him
was it really too much
to be able to depend on
a goddamned vacuum cleaner

there is no antidote
I know that
for clocks ticking, for bones hollowing
but I passed the phone to my little girl
all the same

I heard both sides of the conversation
a grandad, a granddaughter
'What have you been doing today?'

'We planted flowers!'
'That's brillo! What type of flowers?'
'Really, really lovely flowers!'
and so on

after a few minutes
she handed me back the phone
I sensed it, the change
we talked on, a father, a son
the news
the football
the weather
smaller, bigger things, and before we hung up
he said he knew
that it was just a vacuum cleaner
and I felt myself smile
because I knew
that this time he meant it

A Mass Shooting
in Boulder, Colorado

People dressed in ten-thousand-dollar suits
sit in a million-dollar studio
asking loaded questions
about loaded guns

they talk about the Constitution
as if it were more
than just a piece of paper
filled with words
just words
written hundreds of years ago
by other men
in another room

never mentioned
are the mothers, fathers
sisters, brothers
it dawns on me
for the fifth or sixth time
today
that people
will never
ever
change

I pick up the remote
let my thumb hover
over the on/off switch
raise my arm
point it at the television
pull the trigger

Purple Skies,

Pink Sheep, Brown Grass

I was a child prodigy once
for a while
six months or so
I was pandered to, paraded
my head spun as I asked myself
how could everyone know
something that I did not

I liked to draw, to paint
still do
still no good
I had been painting and drawing
purple skies, pink sheep, brown grass
things the way
that they were not supposed to be

abstract thought
being beyond a child so young
they jumped, leaped wildly
to a ridiculous conclusion
and all at once I became visible
luminous
to my classmates, my teacher
myself
for six months or so

colour-blindness
that was all
colour-blindness and just like that
I was invisible once more

Apple Cores and
Street-Corner Small Talk

How will it be after I get old
get older
when my body breaks down
even further
when a voice says
Grandad
while I am still getting used to
Dad

how will it be after she leaves
when she has gone
to conquer the world
when the musketeers go from three
to two
when her room is quiet and finally
finally, tidy

how will it be after they go
when the phone no longer rings
when the visits stop
when the birds
stand on the garage roof
but nobody whistles
no birdseed, no apple cores appear

how will it be when the vaccine comes
when the virus goes
when life reclaims itself
when the world exhales
and street-corner small talk resumes

how will it be after the next wave of tests
when I learn if my eye
is responding to treatment
or whether the trees and the cat and my hand and her smile
are to remain distorted
funhouse mirrors
B-movie nightmares

how will it be after I collect her from school
and she tells me that someone
was mean to her
when I have to gulp the fury back down
when I have to pretend to her
to myself
that I do not have the darkest thoughts
thoughts that thrum and beg and demand
to be acted upon

how will it be after I make a call to the plumber
pleading with him to return
to finish the job
while pleading with myself
to hold on to
even a whisper of dignity

how will it be after I get up to do my run
a lumbering 5K in the cold and the wind and the rain
while thinking back
to when it was easy
or at least
not this hard

how will it be after I finish this stanza
after I finish this line
after I finish this word
how will it be after right now

Different Times

Fifteen years I've known him
the farmer
we chat, the fence between us
a dog at his feet
a cat at mine
once a week or so

today, in passing, this proud bachelor
mentioned
that he had been married
half a century earlier
he saw my surprise
seemed surprised himself
that it had slipped out

I asked
he told me that they had been too young
far too young
that it had lasted
just a matter of months
that he barely knew her then
that he didn't know her now

he told me that they were different times
changed the subject to his brother
six years old in 1951

doubled over all evening
curled, knees to chin all night
vomiting all the next morning

a ruptured appendix
his mother suspected
but had other children to wash and to dress and to feed
there was a knock at the door
the postman on his round
a round that took him near the hospital
she asked and reluctantly
he delivered

a week later the little boy
six years old
was collected from the hospital
once again, by the postman
who reported that a nurse had said
of all of the children on the ward
he gave the least trouble
that he had barely said a word at all

The Drive Home on
Saturday, November 2nd, 2019

The road runs straight
lit only by car lights and the night sky
it is late
or early
depending

rubber on asphalt
I slide into the dips
slip over the rises
the same song on repeat
as always, I drive away, and to

I know where I am going
literally
but not
metaphorically
which is OK

I have something to say
it will change things
it sits in the pit of me
boiling
ready

a dial tone fills the car
she answers
I taste the metal of it as it leaves my tongue
then it is said
and cannot be unsaid

Howls

She was a bohemian
I suppose
people would have said it
with air quotes and eye rolls

part of my life for a short time
she lived here and there
made her own clothes
had a dog with a neckerchief

the world and the people in it
were hers
to save
fair enough

when we knew each other
I barely knew myself
a canvas, not blank
not quite

her hands were tiny
she took my face in them
looked deep into my eyes
told me to howl
loud as I could
at the full moon

I smiled, shook my head
'No, thanks.'
she was not deterred
insisted that it
would be good for me
would open me up
let my wildness out

her hands were warm on my face
I felt my smile waver
she moved a little closer
sensing I was close to cracking
to giving in
to howling

a whisper this time
'Go on, howl at the moon, let loose
you will feel free.'

so, I did
and I didn't

Update

The pop-up tells me
that the laptop needs to restart
that urgent updates require installation
this has happened before
I clicked *restart* each time
with a knot in my stomach
a fluttering thought in my head
telling me that it may not restart
that it may shut down and stay down
resistant to resuscitation
finished, kaput, spent

the laptop contains years of poems
precious photographs
important databases
considering all this
you might expect a certain diligence
in terms of backing up
but backing up
was never my style
precluded by a mix of optimism
trust and stupidity

so I click *restart*
the screen goes black
the knot tightens
the small internal fan slows

stops
I hold my breath
the fan whirs to back to life
the screen flickers
a message appears
Important Updates Being Installed
This Could Take A While
Do Not Shut Down Or Power Off

it is late
I watch the screen, hypnotised
after five minutes the update is 2% complete
this is going to take a while
I stand up
walk down the hall to bed
hoping that it will be OK tomorrow
hoping that I will be too

The Bird

These last three mornings
I have been woken
by a bird
in the attic

I have checked the gutters
the roof tiles
the vents
for cracks and holes
and found none
yet, each of the last three mornings
the bird has squeezed its way in

I creak out of bed
get dressed
climb up the stairs to find him
flitting and fluttering
I talk to him as I open a window
calm him, cajole him
wave my hands madly
but there is affection
in my words
and my hands
and I know
that he can sense it
as he flies haphazardly away

long shot that it is
I think it is the same bird
that has come
each of the last three days
I think it is a he and I think
if he were to go
by any name
it would be Frank

I don't know much about birds
but Frank might be a starling
his feathers are dark
his eyes are beady and orange
he looks panicked and faintly angry
at all times

he knocks things over in the attic
craps on the banister and carpet
causes small havocs each and every day
Frank is a son of a bitch
I like Frank

On the Escalator
in Liffey Valley

I don't drink
have never been drunk
unusual
for an Irishman

in Spain, two summers ago
we got talking to an English couple
spent an evening with them
they drank and kept at it
were amazed
at the non-drinking Irishman
and when I told them
that at home I was famous
I think they half believed me

I have never been drunk
have never stood too close to a stranger
to tell them
with swollen tongue and loose lips
that I love them
have never tried to pick up a pint
only to knock it to the floor
have never walked down a midnight street
shout-singing
on a company night out

have never vomited behind the bins
in a back alley
have never blacked out
to wake up
hungover

but
when I looked at you
that day
on the escalator in Liffey Valley
I felt the whole world tilt

Vending Machine

It's been one of those days
so I decide to end it
with something from the vending machine

wrappers and packets
primary colours
so many, all good

I settle on a Mars bar
put the coins in the slot
press E4

the metal coil rotates
the bar is pushed forward
only to fall and rest against the glass

I should have expected that
Jesus
I shake the machine; nope

then, lightning strikes
I put the last of my coins in the slot
press D4

the metal coil rotates
a packet of Maltesers is pushed forward
I think I might be a genius

I hold my breath
the Maltesers fall
and land on the Mars bar

I wait for gravity to take hold
it does not
the Maltesers sit on the wedged Mars bar

I think, *well, that's disappointing*
then, in the vending machine glass
I see my reflection

Time Is a Rabid Dog

At first you didn't see it
you were so alive
so quick in your step
that it was far behind you
an indecipherable speck
almost nothing, really

you became aware of it later
distant, concentric growls
eyes on you
always on you

later still it came
with such stealth
that when you turned
you saw
only its hot breath
on cold nights

eventually it made its move
the attack wild and brutal
bear-trap jaw, steel teeth
foaming mouth, eyes red-brown fury
matted fur on your tongue
as you bit back
again and again and it fell back
again and again
to stalk, hackles raised

now it sits on your lap
a curled heat
a contented rumbling
under your hand
the television is on
but you don't watch it any more
instead you gaze out the window
at the November garden
and whimper
at the dry leaves on the grass

M Is for Moon

The moon is blue
it is Hallowe'en
in the time of the virus
we walk along the canal
doors go unknocked
doorbells unrung
no tricks, no treats
her mouth is empty
of chews and chocolate

she carries a small light
in the shape of a pumpkin
there are distant fireworks
we hear the bang
before seeing the colour
the smell of sulphur
finds us on the breeze

she suggests that we play a game
'Sure.'
she suggests I Spy
my wife and I laugh
tell her that it is dark
that you can't play I Spy in the dark
she starts all the same
M is for moon
S is for star

C is for cloud
then she stumps us
we guess and guess until
W is for wind

in unison we exclaim
'You can't see the wind!'
I see her moon-shadow shake its head
'Of course you can
look at it ripple the canal
look at it move through the trees
the long grass
Mam's hair.'
I look down at her
shake my head in disgust
happy as I have ever been
to lose

The Alchemist

I was a boy when we met
and he
had just a year or two
left in him

no common ground
at first
until he pointed
at the paintings
on the walls

my eyes widened
his smile did too
I painted but he
was a painter

he showed me his brushes
his palette knives
his easel
showed me how
he mixed his colours
even gold

he wrote them out
the colours, the quantities
on an uncrumpled piece of paper
so that I might make
my own gold

I tried and tried again
giving up eventually
accepting that the magic
was not in me

a few weeks later
I saw him again
he handed me a small glass jar
gold, liquid gold

on the drive home
I cupped it in my hands
entranced by the light
it generated
from within itself
I never could bring myself
to use it
precious as it was
it is still around somewhere

A Rainy Evening in October

Unusually for you
you were quiet
didn't say a word
I said a few things
not much
told you that the house looked well
though it was strange
to see the gates closed

caught you up with family news
the local goings on
nothings and more nothings
my daughter took over then
the little girl who
on the drive over
had been worried
unsure of what to say

she told you about her new teacher
how it is so important for everyone to wash their hands
and to use sanitiser afterwards
how she loves football now and how
her teeth aren't growing
quite as quickly as expected

it was a strange visit
different to those before and honestly
I'm not sure
if we will come again
I'm not sure
if you would want us to

as we were leaving
the rain was falling hard
though it was not cold
and the cemetery gate
creaked loudly behind us

The Truth Is Out There

I slept with the light on
just once
thirty-five years ago I would guess
there had been a special offer
at the church market
three second-hand books
for only 50p
half my pocket money
leaving plenty over
for goodies
I chose a Hardy Boys mystery
The Rats by James Herbert
and a dog-eared book about UFOs
eyewitness accounts, non-fiction
featuring grainy, blurry, photographic evidence

that night I settled into bed
turned on my bedside lamp
and disappeared into po-faced encounters
from pilots, military and commercial
weathermen and astronomers who insisted
that there existed
craft that could defy the laws of physics
flown by beings
advanced, almost godlike and possibly
even probably
sinister

I don't know why it affected me so deeply
innocence perhaps
my mind more trusting, less rusted then
I do know that when I turned off the light
the dark lay heavy on me
pinning me to the bed
paralysed, prone, panicked
the blinds rattled in the window frame
trees creaked outside, though it was a windless night
I felt them lightly touching the soles of my feet
tendrils, tentacles, tongues

with everything I had
knowing that sudden movement could be the end of me
I reached up and turned on the light
my bedroom, utterly normal
empty of alien visitors
ray guns and laser beams
I breathed a sigh of relief
but slept with the light on all the same

Oddball

Tuesday and Thursday evenings
training, under lights
on a pitch in Clontarf

a warm-up, a few drills, a match
nothing to us
then

one evening, I looked up
the sky was a deep, pure purple
the moon was huge
a moon from a picture book
almost reachable
with tiptoes and a stretch

absent-mindedly
with the match around us
I said to my marker
'Look at the sky, look at the moon.'

he followed my gaze
looked back at me and said
'You're some oddball, Denehan.'
maybe I was
maybe I am

Thirty-Six Zeroes

I

Just a year ago
maybe two
I could answer all of her questions
besides the big one
'What happens when we die?'
now I can answer
maybe half
she is quickening
I am slowing
soon we will pass each other
soon I will do the asking
and she the answering

yesterday she asked me
how many atoms there are
in a drop of rain
I told her that I did not know
we looked it up
there are five sextillion atoms in a drop of rain
'How many zeroes there are in a sextillion?' she asked
we looked it up
there are thirty-six zeroes in a sextillion
'That's a lot of zeroes,' she said
I agreed

2

We woke up to rain today
curtains, sheets of it
by the time we got to the race
a blue sky hung over the field
she stood there
in amongst them
younger, tiny
the pistol fired and they were off
she gave it her all
more, even, than we thought she had
finished fourth
afterwards she came to us
wet and muddied
looked at us
tried to smile
and with my thumb I brushed away
the five sextillion atoms
that rolled down her cheek

Boogaloo Radio

on a Late November Afternoon

The worry was syrup
a dark oil behind my eyes
ribboning my ribcage
pooling in my lungs
the worry that I would say the wrong thing
or not the right thing

the DJ had told me
that it would be OK
just two geezers
having a chat
in a room
with nobody listening
except that it was not
just two geezers
having a chat
in a room
with nobody listening

my foot tapped, my leg shook
my heart danced, my skin thrummed
and when I held the poem
in my hand
the words blurred as it trembled
until

he spoke
and I received his words
as aural Valium
felt them land, soft hammer blows
to the back of my skull
felt them radiate
warm and liquid
felt them run down through me
a balm

a lotion

a salve

a potion

and the world became itself again
and there we were
just two geezers
having a chat
in a room
with nobody listening

Roches Stores, Henry Street,
a Quarter of a Century Ago

I was working in the basement of an iconic Dublin shop
long since gone now
it was coming up on Christmas
after hours
we stocked the shelves
preparing for the droves of last-minute shoppers

I was in the glass and china section
unpacking Waterford Crystal
there were four of us
all college age
Donna, Niamh, Ger and myself
the conversation was easy

I unpacked a crystal serving dish
worth more than my weekly wage
I remember thinking
I better not drop this
just before I dropped it
it fell

                        for ever

it had fallen away from me
unreachable for my hands
I leaned back slightly

stretched out my left foot
intercepted the crystal serving dish
inches before it hit the ground

I froze, my arms out for balance
my right knee bent
my left leg out before me
the dish resting on my foot
my weekly wage
intact and sparkling

Niamh took the dish from my foot
I exhaled
Ger and Donna laughed and applauded
and I can't believe that twenty-five years later
I still remember it
as if it meant something

Clinking Silence

I sit at the bar
the barman keeps on pouring
I keep on drinking

he doesn't say much
neither do I
most of what needed to be said
was said yesterday
and all the yesterdays before

still, he checks in with me
every so often
with a glance
I check in with him
every so often
with a nod
it works

it is quiet
a slow night
even for a Tuesday
he dries glasses to my left
breaks the clinking silence with
'My son is not well.'
I did not know he had a son
had children at all
I enquire
'Leukaemia,' he tells me

I shake my head
he nods
I tell him that there is progress
new drugs every day
he looks away
tells me that his son
is beyond drugs
but that they are praying
hard as they can
clinking silence

I sit at the bar
the barman keeps on pouring
I keep on drinking

A Knee on His Neck

Maybe he had been trapped under ice
or swallowed by a rip tide
forced to consider death
his own
for thirty seconds
for a minute
forced to consider that it was ending
forced
to try
to comprehend
the incomprehensible

maybe he had been in a car crash
forced to consider death
his own
the death of others
for a flash
for a minute
for as long as a car crash
and its aftermath
takes

maybe he had fallen as a boy
caught himself on a barb
cut himself with a knife
maybe he had bled and bled
bled so much that his mother feared for him

that he feared for himself
that whimsical wonders
became terrifyingly real
until a tourniquet was found
and the bleeding stopped
after a minute
maybe two

I imagine
all the near deaths
combined
never got near
the cold fear
blind confusion
devastating resignation
of those eight minutes
forty-six seconds
the knee
of another human being
on his neck
while other human beings
filmed it on their phones

Winter Market, Galway

We held our fingers to our lips
took a drag
exhaled
watched the smoke
from our invisible cigarettes
hang in the night air

'I don't know why people smoke
when they can do this.'
my daughter said

we walked on
through the people and the lights
bought some home-made fudge
drank some warm mulled wine

came upon a fruit seller
a strange thing for a winter market
yet the colours were so vivid
the fruit so perfect
works of art, almost

there was a pyramid
of Red Delicious apples
utterly out of season
a heart, between beats, was perched at the top
Christmas reflecting in its cartoon sheen

I picked it up by the stem
said to the seller
'Summer in winter!'

his expression did not change
'One euro.'
I gave it and he took it and he looked away
we walked on
'Some people aren't very happy, Dad.'
I squeezed her hand
took a bite of the apple
it was bitter

Inverted World

I read somewhere that we have mapped
5% of the ocean floor
I checked it online
found it to be true
I looked at the maps
wet, inverted countries
cold, inside-out continents

I scrolled along ridged peaks
rips and cliffs and gorges
straight-line cracks that run for miles
underwater zippers
dark, stark, other-worldly

I saw it mentioned
that we are in the process
of mapping the rest
the remaining 95%
we have underwater drones
submersibles designed to function
in the deepest abyss
designed to withstand the weight
of all of the leagues
of all of the sea

I thought of Jules Verne
how proud he would be
his fantasies made real
but then remembered
how things have gone
since we mapped
all of the dry land
and shuddered

The Mayfly

She looked worried, clutched the book tight to her chest
I asked her what was the matter
'Is it true that a mayfly lives for just one day?'
'Yes, it's true.'
she shook her head
'But that's not long enough!'

sometimes she is invincible
sometimes she is not
I patted the cushion beside me
she hopped up
I noticed how her feet no longer dangled
how they were almost flat on the floor

'Maybe one day is all the time a mayfly needs.'
'It's not fair, Dad. One day is not long enough.'
'Maybe time is different for mayflies. Maybe one second is
    like a week.'
'So, a minute would be over a year?'
'Maybe.'
she was silent

for a minute
'How long have we been talking, Dad?'
'I don't know – two minutes?'
'Two minutes! That's two whole years to the mayfly!'
she sprung to her feet
'I have to go! I have so much to do!'

later that evening she called me outside
to show me huge chalk pictures on the driveway
'For the birds to see!'
afterwards, we watched the sun slide down a pink sky
saw the solar lights flicker on
said goodbye
to the mayfly

Half Lives

She laughed as she said it
'Beggars can't be choosers!'
not that they were beggars exactly
but they were not choosers
not really

they got the apartment
'Two bedrooms!'
for a song
as it should be
with Chernobyl on the distant skyline

she explained how life was normal
how she worked in a bar
in the next town over
how she got on well
with most of the regulars

her husband had left her
and their son
on a sunny Tuesday morning
he died in a car crash shortly after
she wasn't happy about that
wasn't sad about it, either

her son goes to school
gets gold stars
likes art and maths and football
though worries did set in
black butterflies in her stomach
with his crooked teeth
with the rash on his back
with the growth on his cheek

for half her pay cheque
the specialist
took two minutes to say
that they were typical things
for a typical boy

'You don't have to feel sorry for me,'
she said
and I hadn't
up till then
I stood up
turned off the television
long before the credits rolled

Pilot Light

Sleep was butter caramel
from which I woke
into a golden-syrup day
I put one foot
in front of the other
but couldn't get moving
not really

I thought the cobwebs would fall
after breakfast
I thought the pilot light would flame
after lunch
I thought the damn would burst
after dinner

by evening I was resigned
I lay back
into the remains of the day
gave in to the coffee and smoke
lacing the dark-velvet breeze
ready to let drowsy birdsong
faraway engines
and the singing windchime
see me through

then, a blur
from the edge of things
my daughter
running past
moving, really moving
holding something, a doll maybe
laughing
'You can't catch me, Dad!'
and though, these days, she is right
I found myself
jumping up
and I was after her
and I was moving, really moving
once again

Bad Days

There is nothing you can do
about bad days
they come along
and there is not a thing
not a damn thing
that you can do

you cannot stop them from coming
nor can you speed through them
when they arrive

there is no button to press
no handle to pull
no ejection seat
you've just got to wait them out

boil the kettle
make a cup of tea
take a seat
just wait
the bad days
like the good days
will pass

Chimes

I am a son
a brother
a husband
a father
but I am on my own today

the sunniest day of the year
I sit in the garden
reading a book
remaining still
for so long
that a thrush
walks a wing's breadth
from my feet

the phone does not ring
the doorbell does not buzz
no matter how hard I squint
in any direction
I see nobody

the chair creaks as I stand up
startling the thrush into the sky
causing the cats to blink and stretch

in the kitchen I pour myself a drink
water beads on the glass
as I return to my chair
with nothing to do
nowhere to be

I find myself looking at the V
of a forked plum-tree branch
I fall into a stupor
seconds pass
some minutes, maybe

the sound of a windchime
arrives on a curl of air
breaking through
the eggshell wall
of my subconscious
to become the chime
of an ice-cream van
and I am eight again
and none of this is real

Learning to Pretend

My wife and I sat in the garden
watching our daughter
as she glided about
barely bending the grass
a smile on her face
a doll in each arm

we checked in with each other
the way parents do
wondered aloud how we were doing
as a mother
as a father
we wondered what we had taught her
what would stand to her most
as life moved on

it was quite difficult
as she seemed to be emerging
into herself
naturally and regardless
of any input from us

we watched on in silence
as she climbed the tree
then jumped down
removed her shoes and continued
skip-running on the grass

in two odd socks
on to the wall and off again
carrying her dolls all the while

I caught snippets of the dialogue
between her and her dolls
it seemed that they were under attack
running from a jet or a spacecraft
it was a perilous situation
but I had a feeling
that it would work out just fine

A Part of

You've heard them say it
those people
'death is a part of life'

sometimes they say it
with a slightly arched eyebrow
sometimes, as though
they themselves had just coined it
plucked it out of thin air
as though they possessed
hitherto unknown
hidden depths

they say it
in the same way
that they roll their eyes to heaven
and say
'it has to be done'
as if it did
'it is what it is'
as if it was
'time heals all wounds'
as if that were true

they are parrots
doomed to mimic and repeat
phrases and behaviour
without pausing to consider
their words or their actions

I would argue that death
is not a part of life
that everybody dies
but not everybody lives
I would argue that the phrase
catchy as it is
should be amended
that it should be
'life is a part of death'

because death
is the only thing
that has to be done
it is the only thing
that is what it is
and time
is not the cure
but the cause

The Last of the Light

I have watched the sunrise
not often, but I have
it does not compare
not at all
to the sunset

there is a quickness to sunrise
the light is eager, too eager
turning the black to grey
in minutes

there is a whiteness to the sun
a coldness
of colour and temperature

sunset is different
unhurried
those pinks and purples
the whole sky melting
as the sun sinks
in its own time
sumptuously
beyond the horizon

there is nothing as beautiful
nothing worth savouring more
than the last of the light
before the dark

Something to Do

I could not have stopped it
the laughter
had I wanted to
I laughed right in his face
as soon as he told me

after I had calmed down
got my breath back
I asked him why
why sword swallowing

with a straight face he said
'Something to do.'
which set me off again
I tried to stop
I really tried
but the more he stared at me
as if I was the crazy one
the harder it was

he was two lessons in
of twelve
he told me that in the next lesson
he was due to swallow a blunt butter knife
again, I asked him why
if he was looking for something to do
couldn't he volunteer at homeless shelters
nursing homes, any number of charities

he shook his head quickly
had obviously considered this
told me that if he did that
volunteered in a nursing home, for instance
at the end of it all
he would know how to empty bedpans
hand out yoghurts
and not much else
whereas
after his sword-swallowing lessons
he would be able
to swallow a sword

I couldn't argue with that

Barberstown Castle,
Straffan, County Kildare

I dined in a castle once
the table was wide and long
the room was wider and longer
the ceiling had intricate mouldings
and a chandelier

ahead of time I had asked
whether I needed to wear a suit
I was told that I did not
when, in actuality, I did
I sat there, woefully underdressed
in jeans and a T-shirt

a harpist sat just behind me
she played as we ate
food that I could not pronounce
and did not recognise
I filled up on small bread rolls
while cutting the food
and pushing it around my plate

the harpist was an older lady
dressed in a rich, purple cloak
she took a break after half an hour
I smiled at her

she threw her eyes up to heaven
smiled back
we got to talking
a nice lady, local
played the harp for businessmen and socialites
on Tuesdays, Thursdays and weekends
easy money

intermission over, she got back to it
I got back to pushing food around my plate
and watching people laugh and smack their thighs
at limp, unfunny jokes

conversations sailed over and around me
as I thought about how, underneath the ornately embroi-
dered chair, and underneath the three-inch marble tiles, and
underneath the servants' basement quarters, and underneath the seven-hundred-year-old foundations
how underneath it all
when you got down to it
there was only dirt

Late June, Allenwood

Jazz on the air
wending across the bog
finding us from a distance
someone else with the same idea, perhaps
sitting out, free and easy
in the late afternoon heat
picking from the barbecue
aromas thick enough to sink teeth into

I thought of my father
thirty years before
cigar in hand
smoke rising as a straight grey line
up and up and up
'These are the days!'
they were
they are

an ant runs across the table
my daughter doodles under her sun hat
my wife wallows in a half-drowse
the lilting, swaying day, ours
I look up
clouds
ghosts of autumn
lies of summer
clouds
beautiful, beautiful
only ever bringing rain

Mantelpiece Carriage Clocks

'Parkinson's got her,' they said
the first to see me naked
innocently
as she cleaned her bedroom window
two doors down
while I stripped and scrubbed
beach sand from myself
'Parkinson's got her,'
said with a touch of anger
not true, of course
she lived years with it
saw the world with it
cuddled her grandchildren with it
Parkinson's did not get her
what got her
was Parkinson's and time

I lost a friend to cancer
after the funeral we stood
old footballers
awkwardly, under a sycamore tree
somebody mentioned
that he was a flyer on the pitch
but that you can't outrun
the big C
I said nothing, but thought
that he didn't try to outrun it

that the cancer was a part of him
a constant companion
that he worked with
slept with
ate his breakfast with
that cancer didn't kill him
what killed him
was cancer and time

time, that wily dog
rage and blame beading on its coat
falling to ripple dark puddles

time, hiding in mantelpiece carriage clocks
behind ornate watch faces
in the workings of railway platform displays

time, that sneering ghost
who we will meet
face to face
just once

He Did Smile

It is only now, thinking back
that I understand
what he was telling me

people never ask
but always think
'How?'
when they hear
that it was suicide

as if it matters how
when all that really matters
is why

I don't know how
I don't know why
he was good
seemed easy in himself

in saying that
when I heard the news
I knew
what he had done
before the word was said
suicide

it is only now, thinking back
to that night out
dreary conversations from dreary people
the usual
we looked at each other
I said to him, quietly
'I don't want to be here.'
he smiled, he did smile, as he replied
'I don't want to be anywhere.'

The Mystery

I could throw a javelin
wasn't bad at the long jump
but on the track
hopeless

my age group would be called
I would take my place
at the starting line with all the others
the only sound being the blood in my veins
and the starter
'On your marks... get set... go!'

my fingers tight
my hand a blade cutting through the air
pumping arms, piston legs
the unbridled power of my feet spinning the world on its axis

yet, almost immediately, they would glide by
I would watch them
as though I were a spectator
how their vests pressed against them
rippled behind them
how their calves were sinewed
in ways that mine were not
how their eyes looked straight ahead, unblinking

they would sail past and I
would wonder why
we were so different
just what set us so far apart

I remember sitting in my bedroom
one Sunday evening
having finished dead last that morning
I jotted down the reasons in a notepad
maybe they had better gear
better coaches
maybe running was in their genes
maybe winning was more important to them
maybe they simply just wanted it more

nothing was conclusive, so in the end
I decided that it was a mystery
as I took another sip
of hot chocolate
with seventeen marshmallows
chocolate sprinkles and just a dash
of caramel syrup

Winter Yesterday, Summer Today

The call yesterday was grim
he could not keep food down
liquids ran through him
he was shaking
with fear and weakness
my mother spoke slowly
held herself together
while using words like 'distressed'
'upset', 'painful', 'empty'

she had watched him
reach for his chest
she had seen the change in his eyes
as they wondered
both of them
what might happen next

he rallied, as he always does
shooed the ambulance men away
after shaking his head, exasperated
at the battery of tests
at the poking and prodding
he found just enough, as he always does
to push back
against the unknown

the call today was not grim
I could hear her shake her head
amazed
he had slept well
woken early
had a little cereal for breakfast
the day before half-discarded
half-forgotten
himself again

I walked in the garden
listening to my mother talk
her voice was threadbare
another close one
another little miracle
we moved on to the weather
as we always do
I looked up
had to squint
told her that there were no clouds
that there was heat in the sun

Miles Away

It is just after eleven
my cheek finds eiderdown
in soft brushed cotton
I stretch out
hook the back of my toes
just beyond the end of the bed
no aches, no pains
I find that I am smiling to myself

thirty-two miles away
my father is woken
by a thunderstorm
in the pit of his stomach
he sends emergency messages
to his limbs
they respond
eventually

I fall, quick and easy, into a dream
in the dream we are on holiday
my daughter has found a book
buried in the sand
a book about flowers
our faces smile at her from the petals
she smiles back

thirty-two miles away
my father rocks back and forth
on the toilet
his forearms pressed against his stomach
nothing left in him
but the cold
he sees goosebumps on his shaking thighs

I wake at 5 a.m., a bird outside my window
unaware that I am listening
it sings and sings

thirty-two miles away
my father puts his palm
to his chest
as if to listen
as if to ask
was that a flutter
was that pain

we have breakfast together
my daughter and I
we compare dreams
she loves mine
I can make no sense of hers

thirty-two miles away
my father is assuring the ambulance men
that he feels fine
that he just needs to sleep
that he just needs to sleep

at half-past eleven, my mother calls me
fills me in
on the night before
guilt arrives in a torrent
I put my thumb in the dam
as I try to reassure her
with tepid platitudes

she tells me that she is waiting
for the doctor to call her back
I ask her how he is now
my father
she tells me
that he is sleeping peacefully
one hundred million miles away

Another Question

'Why did I cry so much when I was a baby?'
is what she asked
'For food, for sleep,'
is what I told her

she thought about that
'Why else?'

I told her that in the womb
her world was small, was dark
that she could touch all sides of it
rest against it, lean into it
lie on the bottom of it
that she relied on touch alone
to explore
to feel the limits
her own
and the limits of the whole world

then, through no fault of her own
she was born, and like all newborns
she could not see
the world being just a blur of noise
that she reached into
looking for limits
finding none

that no matter how hard she stretched
how far she reached
her small palm, the still-puckered tips of her fingers
felt nothing

she said that it must have been very scary
but she apologised all the same
for her cries, for the worry

tonight, she asked me to tuck her in very tightly
my daughter, the burrito
she said that she liked it
that she felt safe
but that she also likes knowing
that the world has no limits
that the universe is infinite
I smiled at her and she smiled back
'That's a good thing, Dad, isn't it?'
I told her that it was
most of the time

After a Two-Hour Phone Conversation
with Amazon

I stand at the window
the phone warm on my ear
hold music plays
a piano piece on a loop
not bad actually

zero degrees in April
a fair wind
a white empty sky

I am passed around, have spoken
to many different customer service representatives
from many different departments
each one assures me that they care
that they want to help
but they know that I know
that they don't
that they won't
still, we do our dance

their names flit from the exotic to the mundane
from the godlike Vikas, Shashank, Cherron
to the run-of-the-mill Maria, Hal and Trish
there is a Steve too

who chuckles when I give him my name
I chuckle along with him
without knowing why exactly

I learn a little bit about each
Maria calls it as she sees it
that's just who she is
Vikas is able, but unwilling to help
Cherron is willing, but unable to help
Shashank is seeing a psychiatrist
who has told him that singing
will help him *come out of himself*
and Trish hangs up
when the going gets tough

I go out for a walk
to clear my head
the hold music will not let go
so I do not resist it
and as I hum along I notice
that there are cherry blossoms
in amongst the falling snow

Paradise

He couldn't believe it
the dashboard lighting up
as if he'd just hit the jackpot

the car started to slow
and before he even had a chance
to pull over
it lurched to the left and shuddered
to a stop

he got out
looked at it
the way a teacher might look
at the class bad apple
he crossed the road
stepped into a café
asked at the counter
if there might be a mechanic nearby

he was in luck
the owner's brother
knew his way around a car
he would come, take it away
patch it up
if he could

with nothing to do
but wait
he took a corner booth
looked out the window
at the car, the traitor
wondered how long it would take
how much it would cost

'What can I get you?'
he turned, looked up at a waitress
saw her all at once
grey jeans, black T-shirt
long, dark hair tied back
she held a small notepad and a pencil
not beautiful, but beautiful

he ordered a coffee and a Danish
a couple of minutes passed by
he didn't look out of the window again

she returned, put the Danish down
handed him the coffee
told him that refills were free
he spent the afternoon there
the evening too
learning a little more
about her
with each refill

she had grown up in the town
had never travelled too far outside it
hoped to study horticulture

to work outdoors
paint pictures on the land
but fell pregnant in her teens
ending all of that

her childhood sweetheart
skipped town
and the country
a month before their son was born
she, they
hadn't heard from him since

she sketched in her free time
dream gardens, mostly
he asked to see one
she just laughed and shook her head

it had been her day off
but another waitress
had gone into labour
earlier than expected
so she had got the call
'What are the odds?'
she asked
he knew what she meant

every time the phone rang
he looked towards the counter
waiting for the signal
that the car was fixed
that he could go

he asked when her shift was over
she smiled, looked away
said that it had finished
an hour ago
he nodded at the seat opposite him
she put her notebook and pencil
into her back pocket
sat down

he learned that she lived with her father
that her mother had died, cancer
three years earlier
he put his hand
over hers
she let him

the sun set over her shoulder
he watched the light
move slowly down
the side of her face
a kind of art
a kind of miracle

he had a feeling
a certainty
that everything had led to this
that the universe had conspired
or aligned
to bring them together
that it was meant to be
destiny
all of that

as the last of the day disappeared
over her shoulder
he saw a truck pull into the car park
he saw the car on the back of it
he saw a man get out
walk to the side of the truck
flip open a control panel
saw his car lowered
to the ground

the man opened the door of the car
climbed on to the driver's seat
turned the key in the ignition
and it started
it started

he looked at the waitress
she looked back at him
he wanted to tell her
about destiny, the universe
how it was *meant* to be
how they were supposed to meet
not ten years ago or last week
next month or in five years' time
but today, now, right now

he wanted to tell her
but he knew
that it would sound like a line
a stream of clichés
he wanted to tell her
he tried to tell her

the horn honked twice
she looked over her shoulder
saw the car
looked back at him
'I guess you have to go now?'

he followed her to the register
handed her a twenty
she handed him the bill and his change
he said goodbye
she said it back
they looked at each other
until she smiled with her mouth
but not her eyes and it was too much
it was just too much

he turned, walked away
out of the café to his car
he shook hands with the mechanic
thanked him
paid him
climbed into the car and drove

twenty-five miles later he stopped
to use a public restroom
all those refills he supposed
he took the bill from his pocket
turned it over
on the back there was a sketch
a garden
drawn sure-handed, in wondrous detail
it looked like paradise

Impossible Questions
from My Daughter

Usually, it's favourite food
or favourite animal
favourite song or favourite singer

today it was favourite word
'impossible', a good word
is what I replied with

she had asked the question
expecting it to be easy
not expecting it
to be returned to her and so

while I mulled it over, I asked her
for her favourite word
she flitted from 'cat' to 'happy' to 'poop', 'friend-
    ship' to 'worm' to 'mermaid' to 'ice cream'
her voice rising gently until
'It is impossible!'
it was
it is

then, it came back around to me
I told her that my favourite word
the best word

is 'and'
she gave me a look
the familiar look
'Dad, you are crazy!'

I put my hands up
shook my head
asked her to think of *and*
what it means
what it really means

we sat in sunny silence
the cat sleeping between us
it came to her then
'It means that there is more!'
'Exactly!'

we smiled at each other
comforted by the understanding
that there will always be more sunrays and love and spiderwebs and library silence and hope and tickles and spooky
stories and vapour trails and electricity pylons on trembling
horizons and road trips and birthday cake and singing and
questions and questions and questions and long hugs and
short hugs and nothing moments and everything glances and
fingertips and puddles and underwater high fives and shriek-
ing laughter and fireworks and fireflies and

Prisms

We drove towards it
so vivid and so close
as though we might drive
under the rainbow

for the first time
we could see the end
or the beginning
depending

it landed just beyond a field
loud colours pushing silently
into a garden
turning clothes
on a washing line
holy things

'Is that all there is
at the end of a rainbow?'
my daughter asked
from the back seat
'That's all,'
I said

Hit the Road

I was asked by a friend today
what I plan to do
when I receive the vaccine
I told him that I will visit my parents
he remained silent
expecting me to go on
but that was it

until he asked
'What else?'
'Nothing else.'
'There must be something.'
    'Must there?'
he stared at me
shook his head with a smile
I was a curiosity
even to be pitied

he seemed to expect me
to return the question to him
so I did
he lit up, said that he intends
to go to a pub
sit at the bar
order an ice-cold pint
and knock it back
he smacked his lips together
it was quite a performance

he went on to ask me
if I still intended to wear a mask
I said that I did
that I liked the masks
he threw his head back
sending a guffaw skyward
told me that I will go unrecognised
if I continue to wear a mask
I nodded

his eyes widened
he lowered his voice
'Don't you miss human interaction?'
          'No.'
he didn't recoil exactly
but something had changed and he said
that he had to hit the road
and I nodded and watched him
get into his car and drive away

Travelling to Work Every Day
for a Decade

The bus was a raindrop
falling from a cloud that hung
above a volcano
once I got on
paid the fare
sat down
the journey and the destination
were inevitable

I would sit
there on the bus
reading a book
listening to music
watching the world go by
trying not to think
thinking, all the same

the city was a shadow
dark velvet
hungry
looming
a perpetual autumn
a weeping infection
that I stepped into
of my own free will

the Liffey was the Styx
sludged by bile and oil and shopping trolleys
I sat beside it one grey summer lunchtime
watching eels fight
over a discarded cheeseburger
a woman, half my age, put her bag beside me
took off her shoes
peeled off her leggings
and replaced them with a new pair
as if I did not exist
in retrospect, she was right

the trees on Hatch Street were claws
nature distorted
stark and birdless against the building

the building was a heart
rotten and rotting
and we were the blood
and the door was a mouth
a scream, frozen
that, each day, I walked through

Chocolate Spread

She had never liked it
chocolate spread
but he liked to say
that he could live on it
until he heard on the radio
about palm oil
how it can clog up a heart
make it stop
just like that

she was delighted when she came upon
a brand of chocolate spread
that happily announced
No Palm Oil!
not as nice
for twice the price
but he ate it well enough

she remembered the first time
that she found him
she liked to call it sleep*sitting*
she had woken at 2 a.m. to find
that he was not beside her
nor in the en suite
she padded downstairs
turned on the kitchen light
to discover him

sitting at the kitchen table
eyes wide
a jar of chocolate spread unopened
in his hand

quickly, she realised that he was still asleep
and so, sat with him until he woke
confused and lost, a boy again
easily shepherded back upstairs
to bed and to sleep
to wake up the next morning
himself again

it happened once a week or so
from then on
a curious thing and nothing more
until she found him sitting there
at the kitchen table
eyes wide open
without the chocolate spread

she knew immediately
had felt it when she had walked into the room
she looked into his eyes
before she closed them
kissed him on the forehead
got the jar of chocolate spread
from the cupboard
put it in his hand and waited
for the sun to rise

Listen

You can hear the clouds
if you listen
soft white noise
fibreglass crunching

you can hear beauty
fading
in the wild silences
between the ticks and tocks

you can hear the blooming
of weeds
of flowers
underneath the wind

you can hear my love
if you put your head
against my chest
and listen

Deep-Set

Our heating is broken
two rooms cold now
the plumber let us down
we are waiting on another

we build a fire each day
the room smells of smoke
I like it
it brings back memories
that I am not sure were mine
in the first place

the phone does not ring so much any more
the doorbell: the same
the world is quiet
outside and in

I dreamed about my old job last night
more than a decade since I left it
its claws are deep-set
there to stay I think

snow fell yesterday
on the roofs and the cars
the trees and the horses starving
in the small field next to us
my daughter feeds them

apples and carrots
but it is not enough
the snow fell yesterday
on the roads and the grass
on the cemeteries

I am not afraid of death
though I think about it often
I am afraid
of all of this
ending

Telephone Calls

I have had two telephone calls
today
so far

the first person told me
that he doesn't
want to live
any more

the second told me
that she cannot find
a single way
to be happy

it is not yet eleven in the morning

Cream Crackers

Usually she runs across the schoolyard
a bounding, curly firework
usually her arms are wide
from twenty yards away
today she walks
her smile not reaching her eyes

I take her bag
give her a squeeze
walk her to the car ·
she reassures me
nothing is wrong
we drive home in silence

she does her homework
I potter about
the phones rings, my father
says he can't get the heat into him
I tell him to get long johns
he baulks
says they are for old men
he is eighty two

as we hang up I feel a tug on my sleeve
her eyes are large and shimmering
she wants to show me something
I let her lead me to the kitchen

she points at the countertop
I see two knives, a plate, a chopping board
the butter, a box of tissues
her open lunchbox

she points inside it
two cream crackers
a wedge of butter between them
she starts talking, finally
'In school today I found out
that some of my friends make their own lunch
I'm sorry, Dad
I didn't know that I was supposed to.'

she teeters on a threshold of saltwater
I take her in my arms
tell her that I like making her lunch
while thinking that she doesn't have to grow up
not now, not ever
that I've done enough growing up
for the both of us

Light Show

We stand in the kitchen
looking through the patio door
the solar light, a gift from my father
to my daughter
pulls dreams from the daytime sky
to paint them on the night-time shed wall

in the glass I see the ghost of myself
a translucent me, my daughter at my side
I am fatter
balder
bearded
middle-aged

she, what I used to be, not long ago
smiling, wide-eyed, through the glass
does not see herself, not really
not yet
sees only
is entranced by
the light

we stand in the kitchen
the future
the present
the past
and I look through myself
at stars and rainbows

Cautionary Tale

I

I was young enough to be impressed
but old enough to know
that there was no future
not much of a future, at least
in burping the alphabet
nonetheless, I watched
along with all of my classmates
as he stood there
chin tilted upward
proudly
burping
the alphabet

for the three years previous
he had, for reasons known only to himself
pretended to be a dog
a harmless fellow
but a cautionary tale
unfolding before us
in real time

2

He hadn't changed much at all
though I believe
that on television
everybody wears make-up
I had dashed into the sitting room

to my daughter's laughter
a bee to that honey
'I love this guy!' she exclaimed
pointing at the screen

there he was
flanked by two puppets
deely-bobbered aliens
spurring him on
I watched him tilt his chin up slightly
told my daughter
'He's going to burp the alphabet now.'
and he did

Of Service

It was a programme about urges
compulsions, obsessions
hard to watch
hard to look away
it documented a town
built for, and occupied by, sex offenders
Miracle Village, Florida, USA

it also interviewed a man
with twenty-seven convictions
of violent rape and extreme sexual assault
he was part of a project
not quite rehabilitative
but designed to ensure
that he does not rape again

he had been given a doll
an artificial human
a prototype
life-sized
produced at a cost of $18,000
he used it to satisfy
what he called his
appetite

he explained
that afterwards, after the act, he is dead
that only during is he alive

the doll sat beside him
she had some damage
gouge marks, missing hair, several puncture wounds
her cheek appeared to have been singed
she had been given a rudimentary artificial intelligence
in order to be able to respond
with the correct amount of terror
the correct amount of fight
the correct amount of screams
screams that could be adjusted
for volume and frequency
using an app
on his phone

she was asked how she felt
there was a slight pause as this was processed
before she blinked once, smiled and spoke
to say, in a soft, gentle voice
that she was glad to be of service

One-Way Street

I met him on a one-way street
he was driving the wrong way
accelerated when he saw me
the big man in the big van
trying to intimidate
trying to get me to pull in
to let him by

I was in my battered Chevrolet
sky blue to his dirty-snow white
I would have pulled in
any other day
but it turned out
I found my breaking point
that Thursday morning

I drove forward
he stopped
I drove forward until we were separated
by inches
I waited for him to reverse
he did not
I looked up at him
the big man in the big van
he took out his phone
looked at the screen
as if to say
'I can wait all day.'

I tried to wait but it took only moments
for the anger to turn to rage
to turn to fury and I was out and walking
and he was startled and not ready
not ready at all to get down to it
to test ourselves against each other
to die on a damp Thursday morning
for not a damn thing

he reversed
I rolled down my window as I passed
hoping to kindly point out to him
what a dickhead he was, is
and always will be
but he looked straight ahead
as he drove on
both hands gripping the wheel

The Brain in the Jar

I found it on a shelf in his workshop
a brain in a jar
it seems strange to think of it now
strange even to say it
but there it was
in amongst old paint tins
and a bottle of turpentine

it didn't stand out as such
covered as it was by a film of dust
maybe the light caught it
just right that day
automatically I reached for it
but even on my tiptoes
it was too far

he chuckled, handed it down to me
told me not to shake it or break it
I asked him what it was
he said that it was a brain
as he pottered about
I stared at it
lilting gently in the dull liquid

with my thumb I brushed some of the dust away
watched it become more real, more alive
for a second I believed
that it was as aware of me
as I was of it

he told me that he had bought it
at a car-boot sale
thirty, maybe forty years before
A cool five pounds
is what it had cost him
he didn't know if was animal
or human

the lid unscrewed easily
I looked into the liquid
thicker than water
pushed my finger through it
until I touched *it*, the brain
it felt soft, it felt real
though I can't be absolutely sure
having had nothing
to compare it to, then
or now

Sometimes the Whole Orchard
Is Diseased

Even considering the thirty years
he looked different
the still images that appeared
on the television screen
were not how I remembered him
when we were fifteen
when we scrapped with
and against each other
week after week
pitch after pitch

there was fire in him
more than in me
maybe
but murder, impossible
yet there he was
on the national news
looking different
looking pale, looking hollow

back then, there were rumours
strong, sad rumours
I never brought them up
he never mentioned them

but the priest
years later
was sentenced to eighteen years himself

as children we were told of an angel
who fell far, very far, from heaven
as an adult I learned
that he was pushed

Whittled

He rang today
in good form
considering

he cannot drive any more
has lost his confidence
his edge
told me that he comes
to T-junctions and roundabouts
panics, freezes
that when he gets home
he has to remind himself
to let go of the steering wheel

he told me that his reflexes
have gone
that he knocked his cup of tea
off the tray
and just watched it fall

it's not that he loses his train of thought
it's simply that it doesn't leave the station
any more
his sigh catches in his throat

we talk on
he tells me that he saw a lion on television
having five teeth extracted
and replaced
afterwards it woke and ate
an enormous and delicious steak
during the commercial break
there were three ads back-to-back
about starving children
he didn't know how to feel about it all

he was a carpenter once
taught me how to sharpen sticks
to use as arrows
I remember pointing my bow at the sun
him egging me on
the sticks, the arrows cutting through the blue
arcing, falling
landing point first in the garden
now he is the stick
getting sharper still
as he is whittled down to nothing

Edenderry

The rain is fine
fine enough to slip through our clothes
a stealthy drenching
fine enough to sit on her eyelashes
fine enough to breathe in
hand in hand we walk through this old town
in this fine rain

in my boyhood it was summer here
thriving
men smoked and argued on street corners
dragons in blue overalls
the women didn't like to gossip but
sometimes they spoke in huddles
voices low
and once
a shiny fifty-pence piece was pressed into my palm
and I ran chest first up the winding hill to the bookshop

in the sparkling gloom I settled on *The Collected Works
    of Edgar Allan Poe*
and with my change I bought
a scalloped potato
in the hilltop chipper

I perched myself on the graveyard wall
the scallop hot in my hand
the sun melting over my head
salt and vinegar moving all around me and
I read 'The Tell-Tale Heart' without blinking
forgetting that my own heart
was beating on and on
and on

her hand is small in mine
she holds on tight and coasts along
as I did
I look down at her roller skates
and notice cracks in paths
that were smooth and new that summer
she looks up and asks me
with her glistening eyelashes
what life will be like in the future
we talk of robots and hovercars
and holidays on Mars
little does she know
that the future is here
is now

Bullets

From this room
I have fired several bullets
there was no bang
no sound at all
beyond the click and clack of the keys

there was no recoil
no jarring of my shoulder

there was no wisp of smoke
no smell of sulphur
no residue on my hands

but they were fired and they
are still travelling
still hunting

they might not find their targets
until after I am gone
and they are too

the bullets may have little left then
barely enough to chip a gravestone
before falling softly
in among the wreaths and flowers

Ocean Roaring

I had got word to be there
at 10.30 a.m.
I arrived at 10.20
feeling strange
in school, out of uniform
for the first and last time

I sat, with a couple of others
in the same boat
outside his office
we chatted amongst ourselves
pretended not to be nervous

every five minutes the door would open
a classmate would emerge
stiff upper lip, past us
back outside to the whole
of the rest of his life

my turn came
I stood on hollow legs
walked in, sat down
faced the head Christian brother
black suit, black shirt, black and white dog collar
he said nothing, though it was not silent
with the ocean roaring in my skull

he reached for an envelope
an envelope addressed to me
put his thumb under the flap
tore it open
took out the results
of my final exam
the one that we were told
over and over again
would determine the course
of the whole
of the rest of our lives

he studied it with tuts and headshakes
looked at me, eventually, with disdain and spoke
'I had expected more from you, Mr Denehan,'
referring to me by name for the first
and last time in my five years there
he folded the page against the creases
put it back into the envelope and sent me
back outside to the whole
of the rest of my life

Sometimes There Is Only Rage

I stood on a pitch in St Anne's Park
a park full of hundred-year-old trees
birdsong, half-tame squirrels
and all of the blue sky

I saw only his face
it seemed to be screaming
it seemed to be screaming at me
I couldn't hear him
I had somehow tuned him out
his brow was creased
his mouth was wet
his eyes were fury

I can't remember what I had done
to enrage him so profoundly
but with my track record
of causing headshakes and anger
I am sure he was justified

in the silence I found myself thinking
of games we played on the road
hopscotch, rounders, tennis, squares
and football
the football of romance and glory
played under summer sun and autumn streetlights
the sound, the sweat, the joy

I returned to the now to find him
still screaming
two other faces loomed behind his
they were screaming too
he took a swing
I stepped back, feeling the wind of it
the referee sent him off
the match continued

I found him waiting for me
in the car park afterwards
still screaming
I walked to my car
he was still screaming
threw my gear bag on the passenger seat
he was still screaming
closed the door
he was still screaming
as I drove away, I looked in my rear-view mirror
he was still screaming

What to Get the Man Who
Has Everything

His birthday rolled around again
the man with no hobbies
no interests
often no idea, so many years in, of his age

he told me not to waste my money
that he had no need
nor want
for anything
I insisted
he suggested socks
we laughed

in the end I got him a helicopter ride
a voucher that I slipped into his card
told him that all he had to do
was to pick a sunny day and make the call

he called a few weeks later
said that he had been up
said that it was great, just great
that he might do it again sometime
I asked if it was exciting
he said, 'Sure.'
I asked if he had been afraid
he said, 'A little.'

it felt off
a little askew
I suspected that he had not been up at all
that the voucher remained
in his bedside locker

but I suppose
we both got we wanted
I got to imagine him up there
hovering, seeing the world all over again
the roar of the rotors
his heart
fire all through him

and he
got another afternoon
in his armchair

Zipping

She was worried about losing a memory
worried it would leave her
leave her soon
the memory of her first Christmas
her first real one
when no snow fell
but magic did
dusting our roof
our garden
us
when she lay in the middle of our bed
a trembling stretch of warmth
between my wife and I

she wore a little jumpsuit
multi-coloured
with ponies and a castle and clouds along the shoulders
it had a zip
a zip that she pulled up and down
up and down
up and down
until midnight
and beyond
all the way till morning

not long after sunrise
she led us up the hall
still trembling
still zipping
led us to the sitting-room door
the image is freeze-framed
on the inside of me
her, frozen in the air
high off the ground
mid-jump
her eyes closed
her head thrown back
her mouth a smile
the smile

this memory is slipping from her
its grip loosening
its colour fading
she asked me to write a poem about it
that it might not be forgotten
so
I did

Another Poem about Time

Time stopped
at least once
for eight seconds or so

I know
I was there
inside
my inert body
looking out
looking through eyes
fused
slightly to the left
there was no sound
no heartbeat
no breath taken, given

I saw half of the window
an autumn butterfly paused
that crack in the plaster
the cat on the windowsill
paused
my daughter
our daughter
the side of her cheek
the corner of her mouth, a smile
paused

I saw the sleeve of your jacket
blue veins in your wrist
the blood in them
paused
the swirls and curls of your hair
no longer alive
not dead as such
but paused

your neck
open and elegant
your laughing mouth
a photograph of joy

when time stopped
I saw your eyes
I saw the way
you looked
at me
before
it was too late

Do Not Feed the Animals

Tired of walking
tired of seeing
I sat on a bench and, like the animals
watched the people

bored orangutans
watching bored children
watching bored lions

a little girl banged on glass
again and again and again
the tiger's indifference as sharp as its claws

a laughing family threw popcorn at a giant tortoise
a tortoise born a century before
to a world of sun, song and promises

I looked down
wished myself away
knowing then that I would never return

a ladybird landed on the path before me
red and black gloss
that perfect shape
a whole universe

it cleaned its wings efficiently, gloriously
poised to fly again
before being crushed
under the foot of a boy
with eyes only for the melting ice cream
that ran as albino blood
down his hand
and halfway up his forearm

Hallowe'en

I stand in my garden
unsure of how I have got here
the night contracts
the dark inches towards me
I turn and walk to the house
to my home
the lights are on
I cannot grasp the door handle
cannot push the door
my knocks
hard and panicked
make no sound
my screams, the same

I run from window to window to window
I find you in our bedroom
watch you lean close to the mirror
to pluck an eyebrow hair
you put a towel in the linen basket
turn off the light
walk into the hall

I find her in her bedroom
singing, drawing
loving the whole of the world
she wears a T-shirt
with a cat in a cape

her feet are bare
I hear you call
she springs up
pads to her bedroom door
and is gone

I run to the kitchen
I am outside
I am inside, too
typing on the laptop
the kitchen door opens
you walk in together
she shouts 'BOO!'
I feign shock and horror
she looks so happy
you look so happy
we look so happy

I press my face against the glass
breathe out
the window does not fog

Ace

His name was Ace
or so he said
I didn't believe him
he was adamant
we went back and forth
'Nobody is named Ace!'
        'I am.'
'No way!'
        'Yes way!'
'Maybe it is your nickname?'
        'No, my name is Ace.'

he claimed that when he was born
his father took one look at him
knew that he was special
and announced
'His name is Ace!'

I shook my head
he became furious
'I can prove it.'
        'OK, go ahead and prove it.'
'Not now.'
        'OK – when, then?'
'Tomorrow.'

tomorrow came
he walked over to me
smirking and cocksure
reached into his pocket
held out his hand
resting on his palm
was a knuckle-sized diamond

'What's that?'
          'It's a diamond.'
'No, it's not. It's too big.'
          'Yes it is, it's a diamond.'
'If that's a diamond it's worth millions.'
          'That's right.'
'If that's a diamond it's unbreakable.'
          'That's right.'
'Where did you get it?'
          'My father gave it to my mother before he left.'
'Let me see it.'

I took it from him
flung it to the ground
it broke into three or four pieces
just glass
I looked up at him
his neck and cheeks were red
his lip quivered

'My name is still Ace.'

I said that I believed him

Winter Sun

One day she will learn
to make balloon animals
that are not sausage dogs

one day somebody will take her hand
and everything will change

one day she will lose sight of her children
calling for them
over the sound
of her pounding piston heart
finding them not in waves
bit in rock pools
searching for sea monsters

one day she will say
a last goodbye
to me
and I will say it back
if I am able

one day she will turn the key
in the ignition
the engine will wheeze twice
then fall silent
leaving her stranded
in a shopping-centre car park
on a rainy autumn night

one day her she will find herself
crying uncontrollably
as swallows swoop around her
she will not know why

one day she will sit in this rocking chair
and remember her grandfather's hands
hands that made it
more than a century before

one day she will retire
and surprise herself by finding real joy
in reinvigorating
her long-neglected garden

but not today
January 11th, 2021
today
she turns nine

Rockfield Hotel, Brittas Bay, County Wicklow

It was our first, our only, childhood holiday
the grand reopening of an iconic hotel
resurrected from the ashes of a hungry fire

I remember the ornate gold 'R' on the gate
the long, curving avenue, the anticipation
I remember the vans, the tools, the sound of hammering

my father wondered aloud if we had arrived a week early
my mother looked around, wide eyed
I started to drag our suitcase from the boot

the reception was half beautiful
ornate and unfinished
my father spoke to the manager in a hush

there had been delays, unforeseen circumstances
but we could stay
we were staying!

we walked down a tight, unpainted corridor
within our room was a doorway to another
with no door fitted

we had to peel the plastic covers from our mattresses
tiptoe through stray screws, bent nails
I stared out of the curtain-less window, entranced

we unpacked, left our folded clothes on the windowsill
the wardrobes yet to arrive
I worried that people could see my underwear

our exploration began; there were no signs
no paths, no rhyme, no reason
but we were intrepid

climbing over half-built walls
avoiding random, bottomless holes
pushing through, feeling the sting, of hawthorns

we almost fell into an empty, unfinished swimming pool
played several rounds of crazy golf
on a course almost lost to brambles and bushes

we returned to our room to shower
instead of water, a horror-movie soundtrack played
gurgles and choking and the distant bang of metal on metal

we changed our clothes
as workmen walked through our room
carrying floorboards on their shoulders, nodding hellos

as evening fell, we arrived in the lounge
I saw a cordless drill in amongst the bronze and red velvet
an open tin of paint on the bar

a huge, panoramic window looked over all of Wicklow
but it was dark
and we could see nothing

a gigantic circular grill stood in the centre of the lounge
but the chimney was blocked
we sat spluttering and laughing in the smoke

as the night swirled around us
we ate charred food and shook our heads
I wondered whose fingerprints were on the lip of my glass

there was a comedian
that laughed at his own jokes
and we laughed with him

there was a pianist
and he could play
and did, until the piano bled

and my father, ten years without
decided to have
just one cigarette

I watched him suck on it, lost in it
it was the beginning of something
and the end of something else

A Visit to the Ophthalmologist
on December 17th, 2020

The ophthalmologist saw me
just before Christmas
explained that it was urgent
that the sight in my left eye
was deteriorating rapidly
that he had an idea
a new drug
powerful, aggressive
that would help
that he hoped would help

good news
better than the wait-and-see mantra
uttered unironically
by the previous two specialists

I walked out of the hospital
into a damp winter
that followed a damp autumn
that had followed a damp summer
lights reflected in the puddles
I covered my right eye
the world shifted
a swirl of distortion and blurs

the pharmacist had never seen such a large dose
he explained that the tablets were often used
for people with bad hearts
high and low blood pressure
older people
I told him about my eye
that my heart seemed OK
that I wasn't old
not that old, at least
when he smiled I realised
that he was twenty years younger
or so, than me

there was a winter
not long ago
when the snow fell
not wet
not wet at all
but disintegrating clouds
falling on us
warming us
falling

Raining Frogs in Tokyo

The newscaster didn't seem too concerned
reporting
with wide eyes and whimsy
that thousands of frogs
had fallen from the neon skies
of Tokyo

I had heard of the phenomena
assumed it a myth
until I saw the footage
flailing frogs
involuntary kamikazes
dropping, falling, hurtling

most died on impact
small, wet detonations
a little girl was interviewed
who had caught one
in her hat
very pleased
to have a new pet

a small amount survived
taken by tornados
from their ponds and lily pads
dragged across the sky
to land, miles away

on soft grass
in hats
I thought about it for a while
wondered
what next
for the frogs that had made it
I suppose that they just get on with it, really

The World Cup Trophy
at Brown Thomas in 2001

Working in Dublin at the time
Grafton Street just a ten-minute walk away
I decided to head over on my lunch break
to see, in person, the World Cup trophy
on display in Brown Thomas

I assumed it would be packed, chock-a-block
that I would have to stand on tiptoe
to see it, from a distance, between shoulders
that was OK, just to be near to it
a matter of metres away from it
would be a special thing
to me

I arrived, looked for a sign, a notice, a stampede
there was nothing
a man approached me
gave me a sample spray of a new aftershave
I asked him about the trophy
he smiled blankly
I thanked him and walked on

I explored the ground floor
the usual overpriced handbags and nothing more
I took the escalator

figured that I had the day wrong, or the week
or had simply dreamed the whole thing up

I looked past it at first
sitting as it was on a plinth
in what looked to be
the cushion department
a man stood guard beside it
I walked over and there it was, looking newly smelted
warm gold with its dark copper base
and there I was
a boy again
my hands wishing they could take it
cradle it
feel the heft of it
hold it aloft
an offering to fifty thousand screaming Irish faces

then the moment passed and I was standing
on the first floor
of a deserted department store in Dublin
and, when all was said and done
glad of it

The Magic Hill and
the Scientists

There is a hill nearby
it is magic
people come for miles around
to park on it
put their cars in neutral
and roll
upwards
it is magic

the headline caught my eye
a report
explaining the science behind it
I did not read it
but of course
always more than suspected
a scientific explanation

I did not read the report
because no matter what they say
no matter how logical the reasons
how solid the physics
if they were to come
park on the hill

put their cars in neutral
and roll
upwards
they would know
as we do
that it
is magic

French Toast Breakfast

There were years when I felt the tug of it
the questions, the cajoling
the odd social pressure of how
to see in the new year

only once, maybe twice
did I find myself counting down
smiling, hard as I could
with acquaintances
auld and new
I did try to buy into it
tried to feel
what everybody else
seemed to feel

we made our phone calls early yesterday
settled down to an evening film
chosen by my daughter
about a spy
a real tough cookie
who befriends a little girl
it was pretty terrible
it was pretty fantastic

we filled up on goodies
leftover Christmas chocolates
never solving the mystery

of who kept leaving
the empty wrappers
in the tin

later on, as her eyes grew heavy
we did it, we counted down
cheering at the stroke of midnight
'I don't feel any different.'
'Neither do I.'

we woke late today
the world was clear and bright
there was French toast for breakfast
a new year
another new year

New Year's Resolutions

Years ago
I made a resolution
to stop making
New Year's resolutions
it is the only one
that I have kept

last year a friend of mine told me
that his New Year's resolution
was to stop using his phone
for the month of January

in February he called me
on his phone
to tell me
that the month without it
had been bliss
that he hadn't missed it at all
he trotted out the clichés
how he had begun to listen to himself again
how he had grown closer to his children
his wife
how work no longer encroached into his home life
how he slept soundly and woke
ready to grab the world by the tail

I listened to his speech
then asked him
why he picked it up again
why he didn't leave it in the drawer
why didn't he continue
in his new-found bliss

he laughed
long and hard
told me that he had expected that reaction
from me
that he had even mentioned it to his wife
before calling me
on the first day of February
on his phone

I don't hear from him much these days

Another Poet, Another Interview

I read an interview today
a poet
you might know the type
he spoke of himself
almost with reverence

talked very seriously
about 'his work'

explained how he was a conduit
as though he was the first

mentioned 'the muse'
as though they were sleeping together

talked of 'his craft', 'his craft', 'his craft'
of course

he is a priest
and we
the poor unwashed
receive his poems
as communion
on our grateful tongues

he saved the best for last
before drowning
in an ocean
of clichés
patiently explaining
to the interviewer
and the reader
how he takes his life
his experiences
and absorbs them
processes them
distils them
into something else
what a guy

I am writing this poem
on my phone
on the toilet
where I am doing
much the same

The Joke

The workday was over
I had spent it cooped up
with them
they had spent it
cooped up
with me

we marched to a city-centre pub
for some mandatory
company-ordered
team bonding
some mandatory
afterhours
in-our-own-time
organised fun

a round was ordered
on the company
I steeled myself
ordered a blackcurrant
fended off the usual exclamations
'Whaddya mean you don't drink?'
'You're missing out!'
'Ah, fair play to ya!'
with a smile and a shrug

I looked at my watch
not five minutes had passed
I was not surprised
having learned
that time works differently
in Dublin city pubs

it took just a couple of drinks
for the men to move from football
to women
and for the women
to become lip-curling
innuendo gigglers

my drink sat before me
almost full
it had been spiked
by my boss
who admitted it
with a sneer
'I thought it might loosen you up.'
my watch told me that one hour had passed
but I knew better

the night wore on
I knew that I could leave in another hour or so
that I could slip out
unnoticed between the forced laughter
fluttering lashes, spilled beer, giddy apologies
I dreamed of the cold, dark air
pressing my clothes against me

I began to pine for the petrol fumes
the kerbside retching
distant sirens

'You look as though you are miles away!'
'I wish I was.'

they laughed
I laughed with them
as if it was a very good joke

Learning

I walked, ran, cycled, skateboarded
but it wasn't enough
my father took me out
me on the driver's seat for the first time
him beside me on the passenger seat
every sinew tightening
as I didn't check my mirrors
forgot to indicate
stalled
ground gears

my friend was next
taking me on to the motorway for the first time
baffled as to why
I wanted to drive home
to kick a ball instead

an instructor came and went
who did not talk much
about driving
but did tell me that time travel
was real and that Bruce Lee
was still alive

I couldn't learn
didn't have the interest
the need

until I met *her*
the distance from Santry
to Wicklow
too great to walk, run, cycle or skateboard

our daughter will probably learn in an electric car
think it quaint to discover
that when I learned
we changed the gears
manually
with an iron stick

she won't remember her beginning
my hand a white knuckled claw
on the gear stick
all the way
to the maternity hospital
coming up on midnight
my wife, her mother
a mess of sharp breaths beside me
January 10th, 2012

Still Here but Not There

Withdrawing was not a conscious thing
but I did it all the same
withdrawing bit by bit
testing it
savouring it
discovering
that I was happier
more contented
away

I could still look at the world
still marvel at it spinning
at the morning spiderwebs
at the night-time rain tattooing
on the attic skylights
at my daughter folding time in half

yesterday there was an eclipse
we lay on the grass to watch it
the moon inching across the sun
the world darkening by degrees
until the night fell into the day
and the sun was gone
a miracle born from its absence

Bursting

She did not know where he was going
every Tuesday and Thursday
and he wouldn't tell her
would only throw his gym bag
on to the back seat
with a smile
that she could not decipher

it went on for months
he, gone for two hours
twice a week
returning to her
with that smile
until she asked
seriously, for the first time
and he said, 'Wait
not long now.'

she got the call on a Thursday evening
didn't drop the phone
but did drop to her knees
she took a taxi to the hotel swimming pool
it did not take long
the traffic being light at that time

she was met by a stranger
a lady in a bathing suit
a towel draped across her shoulders
he had come to her for lessons
private swimming lessons
to see if he might overcome his fear
his phobia
progress had been slow at first
but he had persevered
had turned up regular as clockwork
every Tuesday, every Thursday
getting through, getting over
his fear until
he was swimming widths, then lengths

he had explained
that he hoped to surprise his wife
to join her, finally, in the sea
on their summer holidays

the autopsy revealed that he did not drown
but rather, his heart had burst
the way that hers never would again

Roll with It

Like Burt Reynolds

Burt Reynolds could take a punch
and sell it
better than anyone else in Hollywood
I'm not sure how I know that

I was playing a match
ten years ago or so
the usual was at stake
nothing
but there was needle
the whole way through
between the two teams
between myself
and the guy I was marking

tackles were made
with a little extra on them
comments were made
smart and otherwise
I was calm
tried to diffuse things
the best I could

then, late on, I received the ball
he came through the back of me
hard and fast

I went down
on top of him
corners first

we both sprung up
he puffed out his chest
clenched his fist
I took a step towards him
hung my chin out
told him to take a shot

everything stopped
time became smudged
a bleeding inkblot
I waited
the players waited
the referee waited
the grass and the breeze and the clouds waited

I wondered how it would feel
whether I could take it
roll with it
like Burt Reynolds
come up smiling
wiping away a drop of blood
with the back of my hand
from the corner of my mouth

the air went out of him
he turned and walked away
throwing, 'You're nothing but a prick!'
over his shoulder
I can't say that he was wrong

Turf Stacks

I sat on her kitchen step
the stove was on
that smell of turf burning
as a boy I would half scramble
half climb
up the turf stacks
slide down
climb up again
I would find spiders
long legged, full bodied
let them crawl up my forearm

I looked at her
she looked the same
on the outside
her insides were rotting
slowly, quickly
and the turf stack
and the spiders
and my childhood
were gone

I looked at her
and she told me
with a glance
and the twitch of her smile

that sometimes
it is hard
to be brave

that sometimes
she does not hear the music
only the scratching
of the needle

that sometimes
she finds herself
shooting bullet holes in the morning
so that the night can seep back in

Tough Guys Don't Cry Over Spilled Milk

They keep coming
ideas, ants marching
in ones and twos, usually
threes and fours
sometimes

I welcome them
receive them gratefully
for the most part
but occasionally they arrive
unwanted
as I lie in bed
trying to sleep
or driving
or pushing the shopping trolley

I can sense them, feel them
germinating, squirming
towards the tipping point
I push them back
with the palms of my subconscious
until they are gone
often never to return

today one came galloping
catching me unawares
as I unscrewed the top
from a carton of milk
my synapses overwhelmed
unprepared, flooded
my hands forgotten
uncoordinated
for a sliver of a moment, enough

for the milk carton to fall
for me to slow
almost pause time and watch
an albino tentacle curving
from the carton spout
a vomiting, freeze-framed mouth

it went on of course, time
the milk falling quick-fast
a long, wide peacock fan of it, but
ever the tough guy
I gritted my teeth
and didn't
shed a single tear

Mirrored Shades

There is such a thing
as mirror spray paint
I had no idea
I plan to stock up on it
to step into the garden
spray every inch of myself
from my toenails
to the hair on my head

with a pair of mirrored shades
I will be invisible
walking down the street
through shopping malls
in the park
reflecting the world
back at itself

people might notice me
as a distortion
a ripple in the air
moving past
they might look at me
but they will only see themselves
which, when you get down to it
is all
they really want to see
anyway

If Anything

Today I watched a video online
of somebody making a sculpture
out of hundreds of colouring pencils
and some resin
a lot of effort for not so much

yesterday I watched a video
of somebody making a butcher's knife
out of broken saw blade
at the end it cut paper
into very thin strips

last week I watched a video online
of thousands of ballot papers
claimed, without evidence, to be illegal
in the past this would have been offered
as evidence
the acts of a dictator
now, it is America
the good guys
or so they tell us

last month I watched a video online
dogs being hung from their necks
blades moving over their torsos and shoulders
skinned alive
expertly

their screaming remains flung into a container
to writhe together
for as long as their hearts might last

last year I saw a video online
Gaddafi on a dirt road
his pleas and whimpers lost
in the whoops and cheers
of his captors
as he was sodomised
with a knife

the year before that
I saw a video online
of refugees with small sacks over their heads
bound and kneeling
decapitated efficiently and calmly
by men in uniform

I don't know what any of this means
if anything

The Choice

Right at the end
with the heat behind them
pulsing to crescendo
pressing them outward
to roof edges and window ledges
they had a choice
a terrifying choice
but a choice nonetheless

stay
or jump

stay
burn alive

or jump
fall a quarter-mile
and burst on the pavement

I wonder how many stayed
I wonder how many leaped
I wonder how many
just before their awful leap
thought that somehow
instead of falling
they might fly

The Nun with No Bones
in Her Hand

I laughed at first
right into his face
I expected him to break
to laugh along
he did not
I stared at him
tilted my head
smiled
waited
he was resolute
did not laugh
remained earnest
said it again, in fact
'She has no bones in her hand.'

his aunt was a nun
almost one-hundred-years-old
flying in from a country
that I did not know then
that I have forgotten now
I asked him what had happened
how somebody's hand
could be boneless
a floppy, jelly-filled glove
made of one-hundred-year-old skin
he said that he didn't know

I asked him if it was the result of an injury
of disease, a virus
or if she had simply been born that way
he shook his head
said that he didn't know
I asked him how she dressed herself
did the buttons
the zips
how she ate, wrote, wiped herself
he said that he didn't know
I asked him if I should shake her hand
he nodded quickly
said that I should

the car pulled up
she stepped out, tiny, a little magpie
she walked towards us
introductions were made
she offered her hand
I took it, shook it
the skin was warm and soft

'88 or '89

I'm not sure whether it was '88 or '89
and I'm not sure how long the school tour lasted
but it felt like the bus dragged itself
down every single road in Europe

it seemed to make sense to everyone
to spend eight hours on the bus
as long as we could stare at a fountain
for ten minutes afterwards

we saw old buildings, old paintings
lots of old things
long since crumbled to dust
and blown from my mind

I do remember visiting a McDonald's in Geneva
they offered a fork with every meal
such decadence
I ate with salt-free fingers, shaking my head in amazement

I remember waking on the bus
unsure if it was late dark or early dark
I remember, in perfect detail, the pattern
of the seat back in front of me

I remember spending more time on the graffiti
than the view
at the top of the Eiffel Tower
I remember taking the Parisians' rudeness personally

I remember secret adrenaline bubbling
at my first sight, in real life
of a pornographic magazine, in amongst the others
and right under God's nose

my roommate bought a *Playboy* featuring La Toya Jackson
held it in his hands like a sacred thing
my own featured an oily woman straddling a pool table
I'd always liked pool

La Toya lay on satin sheets
smooth skin and black hair swirling
she held a thick snake that ran across her breasts
to coil between her legs

I remember thinking that I would like to be that snake
not just for obvious reasons
but because it was somewhere else

Tomorrow

Today is just like yesterday
and I am pretty sure that tomorrow
will be just like today
there will be waking, walking, eating
there will be things to do
nothings really
there will be minor arguments
major laughter
lots of music
a bit of reading
and maybe some writing stolen
from the time between

the phone might ring
it might not
Tom, the postman, might stop by for a chat
or might not
Boots, the cat, might perch himself
on the windowsill outside
staring in angrily
until we feed him
or he might have a lazy day
curled on a chair
not so hungry
dreaming of plump mice and unsuspecting birds

these days
these normal days
where the clock will slow and quicken
where dogs will bark
and the wind will not be full of kites
but full of clothes, drying slowly
I suppose the question is
would I do it all the same
if I could live tomorrow
all over again

I Am Too Old

Too old to be hula-hooping
to be doing keepy-uppies in the garden
in the kitchen
in the hall
in the bedroom

too old to make paper airplanes
with monsters and flowers drawn on the wings
to throw them high and far
each time wondering whether this time
it might make it

too old for social anxiety
for imposter syndrome
for feeling uncomfortable in my own country
my own town
my own home
my own skin

too old to skateboard down our hill of a driveway
with the post in one hand
a slice of pizza in the other
music blaring from the phone in my pocket
the world a blur

too old to stay up until 3 a.m. playing video games
watching infomercials
and online clips of people belly-flopping
from diving boards, piers and rooftops

too old to laugh at fart jokes
at my cat licking his own balls
at the guy behind the news reporter doing the robot
at, sometimes, nothing, or very little, at all

I am too old to cry at a film
a song
a book
a cartoon
a commercial

I am too old
just too old
and yet

Run Throughs

Ankle deep in oil-spill shadows
I would watch them
hurried people
striding past
people with purpose
real people
with things to do
places to be
deals to seal
all that

while my whole life
was lived then
is still lived now
in secret
more or less

just yesterday my father said to me
that we should get to live twice
that our first run through
should be practice
for the second
some days I think I know
what run through
I am on
some days
I don't

School Day, Nine Years Old

The examination room was an unused classroom
we sat outside it
on a line of chairs
tittering as the lady walked past
entered and closed the door behind her
five minutes later the door opened
she looked at us over her glasses
called a name
one of my classmates stood up
a runny-nosed guy
I had watched him lick slick snot from his top lip once
he followed her into the room
staring blankly at the rest of us

to emerge, blank as ever, five minutes later
whispering that it was a standard check-up
no injections
a collective sigh
before the door opened again
and another name was called
and so on
until it came to me

I closed the door behind me
she sat at a corner desk littered with forms and files
I stood a few feet from her
she asked me some questions

told me to jump, touch my toes, cough
a quick eye test
a quicker hearing test
she asked me to walk back and forth
away from her
to her
I did

she asked me to pull down my trousers
then my underpants
with only half a question in my mind
I did
she looked at me
at my naked bottom half
reached out, held it
cupped and stroked it
over and over
her hand was warm
I looked straight ahead
pretended not to notice
as I came alive all over
after a few seconds
or a minute
or a hundred years
she told me to pull up my trousers
and to leave
and I did

Fistfuls

We had been allowed to vote
for the first time
on the destination for our school tour

we blew it in the end
aiming too high, too far
in hindsight, too ridiculously
with Rainbow Rapids
Ireland's first water park
that featured two whole slides
and one small pool

we all voted for it
pretty much
but found ourselves at the National Concert Hall
nonetheless
a gang of let-down boys
expecting nothing
far too cool to be amazed
utterly amazed
when the music began

later that day four of us cycled towards the evening
still laughing
at thoughts of the furious violinist
a frenzied, jerking marionette

controlled by an unseen, mad puppeteer
the furious violinist who played
as if he wanted to saw the violin in half

we talked about the world
our world
just a few miles wide
but a million miles high
we talked about our futures
not knowing then
what we know now
we talked and talked
our mouths closed only
to cycle through curtains of Indian summer flies

later still we stood on the corner
leaning on our bikes
not saying a whole lot
not saying a whole lot at all
the air thick enough that we could grab fistfuls
to throw at the moon

Hidden Depths

Read a poem
count the metaphors
there will be many
metaphors in every stanza
almost every line
the poem heavy with them

we read knowing that the onus is on us
to dig for hidden depths
to dig so deeply and for so long
that the holes are dark and damp and we
are stiff and tired and sometimes
lost still

we are expected to find layers and levels
secret truths and clever insights
between the words and the lines
expected to cup an ear against the poem
hold our breath
listen, in the quiet, for its heart

well, I have had enough of that
so, this is a poem
that doesn't mean a thing

Forty-Five

Here I am
half of ninety
woken this morning
by my daughter
clumsily slipping a card
under my pillow
she tells me that when she is older
she wants to be an astronaut
a hairdresser and a singer
which is good
as she would make a terrible cat burglar

we set out to visit my parents
a surprise visit
my father called me as we drove
we spoke all the way to his front door
I rang the doorbell
heard him inside
telling me to hang on
that there was someone at the door
he answered, saw his granddaughter
and was young again
for whole seconds

he asked me to hold the ladder
so that he could climb on to the garage roof
to cut some overhanging trees
I offered to do it instead
he baulked

we watched him tremble up the ladder
watched him sway in the strong breeze
as the wind left him and he slumped
to his knees on the roof
for a rest

we got him down
steady voices
unsteady hearts
I showed him the clouds
moving in parallax
looking skyward he told me
how easy things used to be
how hard they have become
'No more climbing, Dad, OK? Please?'
'No more son, no more.'

we drove home
made pizza and ate it
laughing along with a sitcom
a storm raged outside
my daughter suggested a football match
I was young again
for whole seconds

with my wife, an audience of one
we played
stood up to
ran into
rabid winds
winds that crashed
into each other
leaving pockets of stunned still
where the world was quiet

for half moments
we played until our jerseys clung
until evening fell
just before we did

we sat at the kitchen table
sucking on ice pops
I had orange
she had lemon
said that it was zingy
asked for a story
from when I was young
I told her that I still feel young now
sometimes
she stuck out her tongue
asked me if it was yellow

this time last year
we were in Spain
this time last year
I went for a walk on the beach
it was low tide
my feet were bare
the sand was wet
I stood at the edge of the ocean
skimmed a stone
watched it
skip

skip

skip

Sun Shower

We barely feel it
the rain that falls
as confetti in the heat

a heatwave sun shower
polka dotting dark
on to our T-shirts

we look at each other
hold our hands out
to catch warm drops

we tilt our heads back
one or two drops landing
in our laughing mouths

later, while we sleep
it will become a storm
to tear the night asunder

The Gaggle

It was not him
it couldn't be
surely the waxy
sunken-cheeked man
was a fake, a decoy

I thought of him sawing
bent over the timber
beneath the low skies
of Mozambique

I thought of his earnestness
stooping to my level
his hand on my shoulder
urging me to read
his favourite book and when
eventually
I did
I read it in his gentle
half-song voice

a gaggle of old women came then
to surround the coffin, chirping
what a good Catholic man he was
how successful his career
the accomplishments of his children

I tuned them out
hearing him instead
talk of his time in Georgia
of his favourite moment
that of a homeless man
with no fare for the bus
being ushered on by the driver
with the words
'On you come my friend. I've been there too.'

the gaggle droned on
I left them to it

The Courier

He was up to a pack a day
but still
could not
blow a smoke ring

waiting for the light to change
he held the cigarette between his lips
took a drag
the small things, always the small things

he had loaded the van
at 5.15 a.m.
before dawn
long before dawn

hard work
but it paid the bills
the van was half empty now
half full maybe

if he got a move on
and a little luck
he would be home
before dark

the light turned from red to green
the world was smoke
he did not move
horns blared behind him

Spray

The sky was grey
the sea was, too
I leaned against the railings
against the cold wind
trying not to blink

the wind funnelled down the neck of my hoodie
as the waves came snarling, white toothed
to crash against the rocks below
I let it

every so often some of the spray
was caught by the wind
and flung
in my direction
I did not turn away

every so often some of the spray
would land
on my lips
it was bitter

I stood there, the ocean before me
the world behind me
thinking back
to when the waves

weren't quite so huge
to when the sea
was calmer
or seemed to be

July 20th, 2022

Not yet the end
of July and the best
of summer
is over

not to worry
there is not a thing
that can be done
for that
for anything

not a thing
to stop the breeze
from blowing

not a thing
to stop the rain
from falling

not a thing
to stop people
from being people

not a blessed thing; and so
I sit and wait
to see
what might come along
with August

Sitting at the End of
Dún Laoghaire Pier

I waited for him to say it
to stand up stiffly and announce
that it was time to go

the sun had slipped behind the sea
leaving us to the evening
our lines had become invisible
but our floats bobbed gently
fifty or sixty yards out

we had caught nothing all day
the way of things for us
there had been long conversations – long silences, too
I learned a little about his childhood
his parents, my grandparents
he learned a little more about me
the boy he had adopted

with evening came damp
with damp came fog
rolling in, surrounding us
a meeting of ghosts
rendering our floats barely visible

I waited for him to say it
to stand up stiffly and announce
that it was time to go, but this time
he did not

our breaths added to the fog
I started to shiver
eventually surprising us both
by asking him if we could leave

he let me ride in the front on the drive home
'Don't tell your mother.'
we stopped on the way
got a bag of chips between us
he picked at them as he drove
the bag was warm in my hands

The Long Walk

She had no plan
no direction or destination
no reason, really
to start walking

she simply stood up from her chair
put on her coat
walked out the front door
walked away, one step at a time

sometimes it felt like a dream
a dream that she would wake from
to discover new surroundings
old ones, too, long missed

she felt like a passenger
within herself
startled at her courage
her unremembered independence

had she locked the front door?
she was not sure, and a smile
found her eyes as she realised
she did not care

there was a sound
distant and nearby all at once
she was humming
a song of her own making

it got dark
it got light again and suddenly
the bones in her feet
were razor blades

she sat down
on a wall
near the docks
far away from everywhere

to a passer-by it might have looked
as though she was waiting
for something or someone
maybe she was

The Duds

I thought I had read them all
but today, online
I found three small
uncollected
Bukowski poems

a little lottery win
on the first Friday
of July

I made myself a cup of coffee
got comfortable
prepared myself
to savour

duds
all of them

pretentious
impenetrable
nonsense

damn

later I wrote a poem of my own
only to discover
while reading it back

that it was clunky
without any semblance
of melody
a dud

I didn't go too hard on myself
anyone can write a dud
now and then

Bukowski
hope springing
even from his failures

Fuck, Shit and Bastard

The older boys had new words
words that I had heard before
but only from adults
or on television

fuck, *shit* and *bastard*

they said them consciously
as though they had practiced
in the mirror or lying in bed
the night before

hearing the words, I became uncomfortable
not because of the words
but because the state of being uncomfortable
is contagious

still, it was not long
before *fuck*, *shit* and *bastard*
came easy
for them to say, for us to hear

I tried them out, of course
saying them to myself in whispers
but back then it did not take much
for God's eyes to fall upon me

there was another word
worse than *fuck*, *shit* and *bastard*
worse than all
according to my father

hate

he would take my face in his hands
look into my eyes and tell me
that I should never say it
that there should be no room, in me, for *hate*

I remember the first time I said it
the barbs of the 'H' and the 'T'
sharp in my mouth
but I got used to it

McDonald's, Lucan,
June 21st, 2022

Somebody asks
what it is
that I write

I ask her in return
to guess
while giving her one clue

in the form of a question
'What is the worst, most awful
kind of writing that there is?'

she laughs, will not be drawn
I persist but she holds up her hands
shakes her head

I urge her on
promising that I won't be offended
a silence descends

into which she offers
softly and gingerly
'Poetry?'

I laugh and raise my arms in triumph
as she raises her brow
her mouth agape

her apologies are sincere and plenty, and I bat them away
telling her that that there is no need to apologise
for the truth

Dublin City, Winter 2019

It was a quick tightening
a reflex
her small hand in mine

I followed her gaze
to a homeless man
sitting on some cardboard
in a derelict shopfront

he was my age
maybe younger
it was hard to tell

we walked towards him
I felt the tightening again
I squeezed back
it's OK

in front of him was a polystyrene coffee cup
I gave her some money
she knew what to do
he gave her a smile
me a nod
said that it was a cold one
I agreed

we walked on
towards the car park
towards a whole other world
she asked why he was homeless
I told her there were many reasons and some bad luck

she asked me why we weren't homeless
I told her there were many reasons and some good luck

we walked on
through silent winter breaths
I asked if she was OK
she smiled a perfect smile
that never reached her eyes
her hand was small in mine
very small and warm

Jardin des Plantes

For many, Paris is paradise
and in Paris
there is a botanical garden
the Jardin des Plantes
a paradise in paradise

founded in 1635
at the behest of Louis XIII
it is one of the oldest
botanical gardens
on earth

within this hidden world
is another
the Ménagerie du Jardin des Plantes
the second oldest zoo
in the world

it was here that a zoologist
grew close to, befriended
a particularly sensitive ape
and endeavoured to bridge
the interspecies gap

the zoologist found a blackboard
and some chalk and drew
bananas, trees and flowers

a stick man
a rudimentary ape

he left the blackboard and the chalk
with the ape
for weeks, and for weeks
the ape
did nothing

until one sunshine morning
the zoologist arrived
to see
nothing short
of a miracle

in this paradise within a paradise
the ape had finally picked up the chalk
to draw the first picture
ever drawn by an animal
the bars of her cage

Does Not Mix Well

with Others

I tell her
that it is better
for everyone
if I am alone

she nods, upset
agreeing
not agreeing

I walk away and keep walking
trying to calm myself
to understand myself
to put some distance
between everything, everyone
and myself

* * *

I see her in a shop window
browsing, oblivious
an eel slips through my ribcage
I remind myself
that it is better
for everyone

not watching my step
I trip on a raised paving stone
landing on all fours
grazing my palms
soaking my left knee in a puddle
am old lady asks if I am OK
says that I am clumsy
she is right

Away from the World

People, everywhere
going where they go
doing what they do

I stay here
hidden and happy
with the cats and the birds

it can be easy
but it is hard
sometimes

my daughter is ten
sees the world
as something to be tamed

I was like her
not so long ago
not so long ago at all

I wonder when
she will realise
that I have failed

that part of me
has given up
already

forgive me, Robin
for finding happiness
away from the world

you see, it can be easy
but it is hard
sometimes

Purple

We lay on the summer grass
hands behind our heads
looking up at the sky

finding shapes in, making stories
with the clouds
she had asked me what colour I would choose
if we could change the colour
of the sky

I thought about it
thought about how sky blue
is my favourite colour
tried to imagine a different sky
time passed

'Well, Dad?'

I told her that it is perfect
just perfect as it is
she bumped me with her hip

'I knew that you would say that.'

I asked her what colour she would choose
I felt her turn her head
I turned mine
she pretended to be angry

'You know that my favourite colour is purple, Dad.'

I chose not to remind her
that her favourite colour changed from week to week
sometimes day to day
that it had been red and yellow
even black
that it was difficult to keep up

I told her that we should be happy that the sky is blue
that there are just some things
we cannot change

we lay there as the late afternoon
fell to evening and the sky
went from blue to pink
to dark pink and orange
to purple

Paper Clip

My daughter asks, again, why her friends don't invite her over
I have no answer
my wife tells me that her job is getting harder
that the traffic is getting worse
the phone rings
my mother speaks in hurried whispers
tells me that my father is a danger behind the wheel
that she is afraid in the car with him
my father comes on
tells me that his mind is going
asks me to sort out his car insurance
I hear my sister arguing in the background
my father puts her on
we have nothing to say to each other

I look out the window
the rain is sheeting
the gutter is broken, and a column of rainwater muddies the grass
the shower went bang yesterday
my phone beeps
a message from the repair guy
he will not make it this evening after all
makes no offer to reschedule

there is a bill on the kitchen table
a sheaf of paper held together by a paper clip
I like the paper clip

it is perfect
has only one job
does it well
I wish I was a paper clip
before I realise
I am

keeping things together
while being pulled apart

The Carpenter and
the Crocodiles

He would come home
usually just before my bedtime
tired but smiling
he would ruffle my hair
sometimes pick me up in his arms
I would sit on his lap in a sawdust haze
we would talk about our days
mine: days of song and colour
his: toiling over the wood, taming it

often there would be blood on his hands
I would trace it to wounds he didn't seem to notice
wounds deep and ragged
future scars
frightened and worried I would ask him how
his laughing answer, always the same
'Crocodiles!
Huge crocodiles, with the sharpest teeth!
I barely made it home at all.'

in the beginning I believed him
put my head to his chest
reassured by the steady beats within
but with time
I found my answer in the whites of my mother's eyes
as she looked to the heavens, smiling

eventually it became a shorthand
'Crocodiles!'
for other, more and less important things, and then
he retired
I moved away
the crocodiles forgotten

half a lifetime passed
almost unnoticed
half a lifetime
for me
to realise
that he was right
that those damned crocodiles are everywhere

Gecko

It was so effortless
the way you stooped
to get a closer look

only when it moved
did I see it
the gecko

a tiny crocodile
a mini dinosaur
an unexpected wonder

the sun on our backs
other tourists passing us by
for a minute, maybe two

we stayed
you entranced
by the gecko

me entranced by you
I remember
I remember everything

The Thief

It had been a long time
fifteen years, maybe twenty
she looked much the same
as she half walked, half ran
across the road
smiling, waving
at me

it had been fifteen years, maybe twenty
for a reason
for many reasons
that came hard and fast
'I haven't seen you in so long!'
'How are you?'
'Where did you go?'
'What have you been up to?'
'Didn't you have a little girl?'
'They grow up so fast, don't they?'
'This Covid thing was hard, wasn't it?'
'Not to mention the war in Ukraine!'
'That Putin fellow, Lord God Almighty!'
'Are you still in Kildare?'
'Are you near Newbridge?'
'Naas?'
'Ah yes, I know Allenwood!'
'Do you know the Byrnes?'
'Colette and Jimmy?'

'Colette and Jimmy Byrne?'
'They have a disabled boy. Very sad.'
'What are the schools like near you?'

she looked over my shoulder
'Better dash, that's my bus!'
'Do you still have my number?'

'I do.'

I didn't

as I moved to let her pass
she asked, with half a shrug
half a smile
'Where does the time go?'
as if she didn't know

Drunk on a Sip

I reached into my pocket
took out my money
paid the bus conductor
the others did the same

we climbed the stairs
steep steps, half spiralled
to sit
down the back

from Santry to Whitehall
Whitehall through Drumcondra
until we touched down
in Dublin City

we had been there before
but never alone
never without our parents
it looked different, bigger, taller

I don't remember what we did
just wandered, probably
the cinema, maybe
but I do remember the taste

that first taste of adulthood
all of us
drunk on a sip
we didn't know a thing

A Cold Cordial
on a Warm Day

Sometimes happiness is nothing more
than a cold cordial
on a warm day

sometimes the pinnacle of ambition
is putting one foot
in front of the other

sometimes love
is a raised voice

sometimes hate
is a whisper

sometimes inspiration is found in the weed
growing from a crack in the path

sometimes joy comes hard and fast
rising through us
from the soles of our feet
for not much of a reason at all

sometimes sadness is a smile

WhatsApp Messages

Yesterday I got a message
from an old friend on WhatsApp
leading to the following brief exchange

'The Batman verdict?'

　　　　　'I haven't seen it yet… Well?'

'Different to Nolan's take… Noir take
moody broody… not sure I get Colin
Farrell's casting… he looks like a fat
Robert DeNiro.'

　　　　　'Yeah, I thought that was weird
　　　　　all right. They should have just got
　　　　　Danny DeVito back. He'd have
　　　　　done it for a fiver.'

yesterday was March 5th, 2022
the previous exchange between us
had been on December 29th, 2019

he is one of my closest friends

One Small Step

He stood at the edge of the river
not much of a flow to it now
looked at the moon reflected
remembered when he had said in class
that he was going to be an astronaut
how the laughter had been long and loud

he was ankle deep before he felt it
searing wet cold that ran up his back
to nestle at the base of his skull
another step brought the water to his knees
another to his thighs, to his waist
he thought of the cash in his pocket
softening and coming apart
he thought of his phone short-circuiting
not to worry
all that mattered
was getting to the moon

two more steps brought a gasp
as the water reached his chest
one small step
to the middle of the river
to the moon
the water reaching the underside of his face
cupping his chin, his jaw

he stood in the river, in the moon
waited to adjust to the iron cold
the temperature on the moon
could fall to hundreds of degrees
below zero
he remembered that

he slouched, just an inch or two
until the water reached his cheeks
just below his eyes
until all that he could see
was the pure ice white of the moon
he remembered too
a childhood yearning
for weightlessness
he had always wanted to know
how that would feel
so he lifted his feet
bent his knees
and found out

Chrysalis

There was no one big thing
that drove him to it
nor a multitude of smaller things

it simply made sense
at the time
to buy two dozen bottles of water
some granola bars and popcorn
to barricade himself into his room
turn off his phone
take off his clothes
climb into bed
to pull up the covers
to wait

slowly, or quickly
time became an elastic thing
days became blinks
blinks became days

after two weeks
he drained the last of his water
dressed himself
in clothes that seemed to have got larger
and emerged
into a world
that was just the same

Ochophobia

Ochophobia is the fear of cars
it is a real thing
a very real thing
for an old friend

we would meet up once, twice a year
usually
but a year went by
then two
without his call

I dialled his number
he picked up
same as ever
we talked a while
the usual stuff, nothing and everything
I suggested meeting in our usual spot
he asked if we could meet somewhere else
a park, walking distance from his place
sure, no problem

we sat on a bench
a pigeon with a limp walked back and forth
back and forth
the conversation was just the same
nothing and everything

back and forth
he looked all right
a little older, a little tired maybe

he mentioned it then, *ochophobia*
explained it to me
I thought he was joking at first
he wasn't
we talked on, both of us looking at the limping pigeon

he had felt the fear coming slowly in the beginning
pins and needles at the back of his mind
eventually becoming spikes and nails
at the front
he shook his head
knew how it sounded
told me that most of the time he was fine
that most of the time he is not afraid
but that some of the time
he is
that some of the time a white fear descends
and air is short and he breathes in gasps
that he feels as though his heart will burst in his chest
that his hands shake and that he knows
that he knows the cars will get to him sooner or later
they will find him and mow him down
or pin him to a wall
crushing last breaths from him
turning his hips to dust
pulping his organs

I didn't know what to say
we had played football together
he had been a lion on the pitch
fearless, relentless, fighting to the last
I suggested time away from it all
offered to go with him
we sat in silence for a while
the pigeon flew away

three weeks later we rented a log cabin
a fisherman's retreat
two dozen cabins sprinkled around a forest lake
no cars for miles
silence
he was good, good as ever
not much for fishing, we sat on the lakeside
nursing cups of tea
watched the fish hop
rooted for them and against the fishermen
he was good
until the last night

he woke me wailing
high pitched, quiet but loud in the silence
I found him sitting on the edge of his bed
looking at the closed curtains
rocking stiffly
I tried to talk to him
but what could I say
he could hear the engines
couldn't I hear them too?
they were coming

through the trees
they were coming for him
and not a damn thing could be done about it

I visited him twice
in a place for broken and breaking people
it was sad
he was the same, the very same
but different
the conversation ebbed and flowed
nothing and everything
just the same
back and forth
he mentioned the pigeon with the limp
we laughed
he wondered what had become of it

he told me that he still heard the engines
especially at night
he called them *episodes*
he told me that they take good care of him
that he hoped to be well soon
that he hoped to get out

I tried to visit him again
he wouldn't see me
I explained to the nurse that I was a friend
that we used to play football together
that he was a lion
but he had left instructions
clear instructions
No Visitors

I phoned a couple of times
same thing
No Calls
the receptionist seemed nice
I asked how he was
but she was not allowed to say
I asked her to give him my regards
she said that she would
I asked if they were taking good care of him
she said that they were
I told her that he had been a lion once

Best Man

We had grown up together
been in school together
gone away together
he had been my best man
we had not seen each other in years

he had bought a house
changed jobs
got married
made his way

he had got in touch
asked us over
my wife drove
I used my phone to navigate

we knocked on the door
footsteps
he answered
older, balder, fatter
like myself

introductions were made
small talk was talked
the takeaway arrived and we sat
at a large oak table

we commented on the food
reminisced a little
the conversation dwindled
before I asked his wife
what kind of music she liked

he sneered
'Don't tell him. He's a music snob.'
the air tightened
I bristled
while knowing
it was probably true

she smiled, answered
Celine Dion
fuck
fuckfuckfuck

seconds passed as minutes
I said that she sure can belt them out
we haven't seen them since

Millennia

In a few minutes
I am going outside
to read my book
in the sunshine

in a few days
we will pay a visit
to my parents

in a few months
one year
will become another

long, but not too long
after that
the twenty-first century
will become the twenty-second

a little further on again
one millennium
will fall
to the next

with each measure of time
we hurtle slowly
into the sun
we may as well be happy

Mathematics

He did not look like a mathematician
but that
is what he said
he was

green fields and grey towns
their beginnings, their endings
blurred by the train window

I cursed the fact
that I had forgotten my book
when he started to talk
talk that might aspire
to one day
be defined as small

we went through it all the same
the weather, holidays
Covid, family
before we came upon it
jobs

he said that he could express anything
as mathematics
his party piece
he told me
with a theatrical eye roll

'OK, how about love?'
'Beats per minute.'

quick as a flash
pretty good, but maybe
an obvious test

'OK, what about hate?'

the Dublin coast passed by
I thought I had him beat, or that
perhaps he had forgotten
or drifted off
until a nudge at my elbow

'Hate equals love
plus time.'

like I said, pretty good

Five or Fifty-Five

She was holding a box of chicken nuggets
when I came upon her
on the frozen food aisle

I walked behind her
softly as I could
praying that my trolley
would not squeak

'Steve, is that you?'
damn

we killed a few minutes
five or fifty-five
it was hard to tell

she asked me how I was
I said that I was fine
she asked me how we had been
during these strange times
I said that we'd been fine
she asked me how my father was
I said that he was fine
she said that it was a lovely day
that the whole world is well
when the sun is shining
I said that I agreed

driving home
I found myself smiling
at how sometimes
the lies
come thick and fast and easy

Emergency Room
at the Hermitage

I limp-shuffled to the reception desk
a lady (late twenties, early thirties)
told me go to the lower ground floor

I creaked down two flights of stairs
where another lady (thirty-ish)
told me to take a seat and wait

several minutes later a third lady
(mid-twenties)
gave me a form to fill out

half an hour later a nurse (early twenties)
took me to a room behind a curtain
took my blood pressure
gave me a small tub for a urine sample
and was gone

a doctor arrived shortly after
(thirty, thirty-five)
he told me to strip to my underwear
put on a gown and lie on a bed
he asked me questions
prodded, pulled and poked

finding no pain
until he twisted my knee
and I yelped

he took some notes
said that a bulging disk
was his best guess
that it was not uncommon
in people my age
that we would know more
after a scan

I got dressed and reported to Radiology
a man (thirty or so)
scheduled the scan
wrote the details
on a little card and handed it
with a smile
to me (forties)
(mid-forties)
(mid-to-late forties)

The Spot

To get to The Spot
we had to drive over a hill
the road was steep
the corners sharp
so sharp
that you had to slow
to walking pace to take them

you learned of The Spot
from your father
years before
before it all fell apart
between you both
before you let him go and he
didn't seem to notice

we took the rods and tackle
to the edge of the pier
bated up
casted out
the fish were hopping as the sun set
you looked at me
'Just a matter of time.'

we sat there bating and casting
until just before midnight
between us, catching nothing

fine by me but you
were quiet
as we packed up
as we drove back to the house

I never wanted to catch anything
that didn't matter
just killing time, that's all
it's been ten years
longer, probably
you might not remember now
that's OK

The Band

A house party
miles away
a band
that somehow sounded
as if it was in our garden
which was not good
because they were very bad

the guitarist had one riff
and did not use it sparingly
the singer sung entirely without personality
without even a trace of joy
the sonic equivalent of a beige cardigan
a Toyota Corolla
soup
the drummer played angry
trying to beat the drumkit to death
as if it owed him money
or had stolen his girl

they played the usuals
the clichés
Thin Lizzy and The Monkees
Abba and The Clash
'Smells Like Teen Spirt'
followed by 'Walking on Sunshine'
as Kurt Cobain spun in his grave

the moon was full
stark, pure
I made a pistol with my hand
pointed my finger
pulled the trigger
severing the string
that had held it in the sky
watched it fall to earth
the music stopped
the world shuddered
then was still
I got back to reading my book

Maybe All Poems Should
Be Burned

Li Po was born
before many things
in the year 701

a great poet
immortal
through his words

words, poems
that have survived
time and other things

however, his most famous poems
are those
that did not survive

destroyed by Li Po himself
he would fold them into paper boats
place them on the Yangtze river

and set them alight
drinking wine as he watched them
sail, burning, away

those poems
let's be honest
must have been terrible

End

The bridge is burning even as I cross it
the heat on my back presses me on
and light is flung before me
to push into the black

I reach the other side and turn to watch
the bridge falls, flaming
in silent pieces to the waiting water
I know what this means: it is over

I am surprised to find that it is beautiful
but then I remember
that fire and endings always are

Acknowledgements

'Broken Nail' previously published in the *Close Up* anthology by Orchard Lea Books in 2022

'anonymouse_weezil' & 'Mirrored Shades' previously published by Mono. in 2022

'On the Escalator in Liffey Valley' previously published by *Better Than Starbucks* in 2021

'Vending Machine' & 'Telephone Calls' previously published by *The Opiate* in 2021

'Time Is a Rabid Dog' previously published by *Schuylkill Valley Journal* in 2021

'M Is for Moon' & 'Hallowe'en' previously published by *Dreich Magazine* in 2021

'The Alchemist' previously published by *The Pomegranate London* in 2021

'A Rainy Evening in October' previously published by *Freshwater Journal* in 2021

'The Truth Is Out There' previously recited on Mark Nevin's *Dad Pill* (Boogaloo Radio) in 2021

'Thirty-Six Zeroes' previously published by *Plainsongs Journal* in 2020

'Roches Stores, Henry, a Quarter of a Century Ago' previously published in the second *Loft Books Anthology* in 2021

'A Knee on His Neck' previously published in the *2020* anthology by Black Dog & One-Eyed Press in 2021

'Winter Market, Galway' & 'French Toast Breakfast' previously published by *Capsule Stories* in 2021

'Half Lives' previously published by *Fresh Words Magazine* in 2022

'Mantelpiece Carriage Clocks' previously published by *The Madrigal* in 2021

'Light Show' previously published in the Light issue by Paddler Press in 2022

'Of Service' previously published by *Westerly Magazine* in 2021

'Edenderry' previously published by *The Same Page* in 2021

'What to Get the Man Who Has Everything' previously published by Albany Poets in 2021

'Zipping' previously published in *Issue 19* by Rough Cut Press in 2020

'Do Not Feed the Animals' previously published in *There Is No Planet B* by Stafford Green Arts Festival in 2021

'Ace' previously published by Louisiana Literature in 2021

'Rockfield Hotel, Brittas Bay, County Wicklow' previously published in *Fevers of the Mind Press Presents the Poets of 2020* anthology in 2021

'Hidden Depths' previously published by *The Soap Box* in 2022

'Paper clip' previously published by *Púca Magazine* in 2022

'The Carpenter and the Crocodiles' (winner of the Anthony Cronin Poetry Award) first published by the Wexford Literary Festival in 2021

Steve Denehan

Steve lives in Kildare in Ireland with his wife Eimear and daughter Robin. He is the author of two chapbooks and four poetry collections. Winner of the Anthony Cronin Poetry Award and twice winner of the *Irish Times*' New Irish Writing, his numerous publication credits include *Poetry Ireland Review* and *Westerly*.